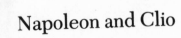

Napoleon and Clio

Napoleon and Clio:

Historical Writing, Teaching, and Thinking
During the First Empire

June K. Burton

Carolina Academic Press
Durham, North Carolina
1979

77- 88659

1907 was a wonderful year

gratefully
to
M.L.K.
and
H.T.P.

Contents

Preface

The literary and cultural history of the Napoleonic era in France has largely been ignored, perhaps because of the persistent notion that the age was intellectually barren. The work of the legions of political and military historians who have concentrated their research on this period has not shown what Imperial intellectuals and historians thought about the history of their own country. The purpose of this study is to fill part of this void by examining how history was written and studied in France during the Consulate and Empire. In the process of examining the writing of history during the age of Napoleon, I encountered other questions, which this study seeks to answer: What really were Napoleon's ideas about history? Did historians conform to his ideas or work independently of the dictator? Finally, did Napoleon or his historians contribute anything to the development of history as a quasi–scientific discipline as we in the twentieth century understand it?

Napoleon's historians functioned in an intellectual milieu established by their predecessors before the French Revolution. In the seventeenth century, educators allotted either no place or only a minor role in the high-school curriculum to history because it concerned the real world surrounding the child. Père Joseph de Jouvency[1] advised against the study of French history except during vacations. While the Jesuits devoted about a half-hour each week to history, Charles Rollin[2] saw no reason for the inclusion of any modern history in the curriculum. In the Oratorian Schools and in the Little Schools of Port-Royal, however, classical as well as French history was an important part of the education of boys.

Several arguments were then accepted to account for the state of the historical discipline. Historians who agreed with Bishop Jacques-Bénigne Bossuet treated history from an ahistorical viewpoint, seeing it as a reflection of the transitoriness and vanity of life in this world, and pointing out that eternity is what really matters. In a similar vein, others expressed concern about teaching any subject that was considered too agreeable, lest students become involved in this-worldly pleasures. On the other hand, Père Clément Buffier[3] considered history as a few facts that students need only memorize but not reflect upon. Père Bernard Lamy[4] saw no need to teach it in formal classes with a teacher because he thought it was too easily learned independently. Nevertheless, Bossuet's belief that history was beneficial in the education of those who might eventually govern was widely accepted. However, because history was confined to the description of great men, great battles, and great vices and virtues instead of the totality of human experience, its subject matter was primarily aristocratic and psychological. Hence, for Rollin history was philosophy teaching by example, as it had been for Plutarch.

Two major obstacles, therefore, obstructed the development of history as a meaningful part of the seventeenth–century curriculum—the persistence of an otherworldly orientation in education and the fact that history had not developed to the point of being a quasi–scientific discipline deemed worthy of respect in its own right. Both a societal revolution and a revolution within historical studies were needed before pedagogues possessed the prerequisite confidence in humanity and government to make history a permanent part of the modern, secular school curriculum.

Naturally, many seventeenth-century ideas continued in vogue during the following century. In fact, annals and chronology, formats that had thrived even in classical antiquity, still appeared. Most enlightenment historians agreed with the humanist idea of the unity of history and progress, and they still accepted the definition of history as philosophy teaching by example. The pragmatic view of history that had been especially popular in the sixteenth century, that historians should work to create records of memorable events as monuments of the preeminence of their own times, was revived and widely held. While some authors painted an overly-rosy picture of the past, others criticized the crimes and follies of former times of ignorance and

barbarism, notably the Middle Ages. However, the great eighteenth–century *philosophes* such as Denis Diderot, Jean Le Rond
D'Alembert, and Louis-Réné Caradeuc de La Chalotais argued
that history should not be viewed as progressing from creation
toward eternity; instead, it should be studied in reverse order
beginning with a survey of the present and regressing toward
ancient times. Voltaire particularly emphasized the importance
of studying modern history since the Reformation because he
believed that it was more relevant and the sources for it less
fabulous. The exemplary works of Charles de Secondat the Baron
de Montesquieu, Voltaire, and William Robertson included a
broader range of information about economic, social and cultural
history as well as about non-Western civilization, all integrated
into the context of the times to form a coherent whole. By the
1780s, the philosophers had expounded their views so successfully that a conglomeration of both complementary and contradictory explanations of historical causation was popular. Divine
Providence, human nature, the great–man theory, national
character, chance, the spirit of the times, climate, geography,
religion, and government were some of the factors mentioned.
While the *philosophes* thus failed to revolutionize historical
studies, they stimulated a dialogue about generally accepted,
long–forgotten but now revived, and novel historical ideas that
eventually provided the modern orientation to historical thinking,
writing, and teaching.

The shifting current of intellectual ideas was not as evident in
the publication of prerevolutionary history textbooks. Although
formats varied, chronology, catechism, and verse were favored
by many eighteenth-century authors and teachers. Often teachers
simply dictated notes to their students because of the scarcity and
costliness of printed materials. The standard and rather arid
elementary works by Rollin, Buffier, Père Gabriel Daniel,
Charles Hénault, Abbé Gabriel Bonnet de Mably, Abbé Paul-
François Velly, and Abbé Claude Millot were those most familiar
and most frequently consulted by instructors prior to the Revolution.

It was in matters of curriculum that the real challenge to

previous practices came from pragmatic, anticlerical intellectuals and politicians. They proposed that the French monarchy should assume responsibility for educating members of society, thereby displacing the monopoly of the religious congregations. More-over, they believed optimistically that a subject like history, which could bring joy to the child, might ultimately lead to his becoming a happier adult populating a more ideal society. Thus, the study of history could serve the fatherland by contributing to the moral formation of individuals. After the expulsion of the Jesuits from France in 1762, the *parlementaires* actively joined the reform movement in education[11] that preceded the revolutionary outburst and continued during the Napoleonic era. As part of the movement calling for drastic change, Barthélemy-Gabriel Roland d'Erceville[12] and La Chalotais urged the monarchy to establish a national educational system with trained lay leaders and official textbooks published by the government for use in all schools. Such is the background for the ideas and developments presented in this study.

This work is based primarily on Napoleon's voluminous correspondence and on the history books and textbooks that were written and published in France between 1799 and 1815. The many scholars who paved the way for this enterprise are cited in the footnotes. Several chapters, however, could not have been written without Henri Monglond's *La France révolutionnaire et impériale* which, along with *Le Journal général de la littérature de France*, was an invaluable bibliographical aid. Sometimes, I followed the contemporary practice of not using authors' long surnames to avoid excessively monotonous passages; and in a few instances these simply could not be identified. If the author of a work which originally appeared anonymously was penciled on the title page of the copy in the Bibliothèque Nationale, I used that name to identify the book in the footnotes and bibliography.

I am grateful for help from the staffs of the Bibliothèque Nationale, the Archives Nationales, the Bibliothèque Mazarine of the Institut de France, the University of Georgia Library, and the Bierce Library of the University of Akron, where the research for this book was done. A teaching assistantship at the University of Georgia financed my first research trip to Paris, a faculty research grant from the University of Akron provided plane fare for the second, and a teaching program of the Buchtel College of Arts and Sciences provided the final one.

I would like especially to thank Ulane Bonnel and Marcel Dunan for their help and encouragement in Paris. My major professor, Lee B. Kennett, originally gave me the topic and, as he once said jokingly, "launched me" into the profession. Don R. Gerlach and Barbara B. Reith read the manuscript for style. For several years, the directors and many of the participants in the annual meetings of the "Consortium on Revolutionary Europe (1750–1850)" have given me incentive to persist by treating a novice as an equal and a *chère collègue*. I am grateful to all of them and hope that the present work reflects at least to a slight degree the high quality of scholarship these historians represent.

Napoleon and Clio

Napoleon's Idea of History

Many of the historical ideas Napoleon espoused as a public figure from 1797 to 1815 had been developed during his youth. As a child at Ajaccio he discovered the past of his native Corsica and of the classical Mediterranean world.[1] While attending the French preparatory school at Brienne from 1779 to 1784, he read some histories of Corsica[2] and learned about the history of his adopted country. In addition, he acquired rudimentary knowledge of modern history as it was then known. Thus, at an early age, in school, at home, and with his playmates Napoleon began to develop his awareness of history.

A prominent aspect of Napoleon's mentality was his early identification with Corsican history. He accepted the foreign identity thrust upon him as an outsider attending the school on a scholarship and responded in anger to his playmates' taunts by threatening one day to aid Pasquale Paoli in successfully overthrowing French control of his home island. His identification with Corsican history and politics, in which his family's fortunes were so embroiled, continued after he left Brienne for the Royal Military College at Paris at the age of fifteen. As in his childhood, he indulged himself in what had now become teenage fantasies of Corsican liberation and glory. Once he assumed his military duties as an artillery officer, he continued to spend most of his off-duty hours reading and taking notes on history. During the second leave, which he spent in Corsica, Napoleon met Paoli and asked him for documents to use in composing a history of the island. But his hero refused to waste precious time and energy searching through archives. Furthermore, Paoli dismissed the importance of Napoleon's historical efforts as being useless because of his conviction that history was not for young men to write.[3] Never-

theless, some time during the succeeding two years Napoleon
completed his manuscript of a Corsican history, and Abbé Guil-
laume-Thomas-François Raynal, to whom he sent it for approval,
did encourage him to persevere as a historian.[4]

The young Napoleon enjoyed the study of history because it
gave him a feeling of power. His customary method was to read
pen in hand and to make notes or abstracts of entire works.
Among the famous books which he used while he was attached to
the La Fère regiment at Auxonne were Rollin's *Histoire ancienne*,
Raynal's *L'histoire du commerce des deux Indes*, Mably's *Observations sur l'histoire de France*, and others by such lesser-known
historians as Abbé Augier de Marigny,[5] Abbé Joseph-Marie
Terray,[6] and François Baron de Tott.[7] His manner of working on
these was to first read a portion of the book before turning back to
begin taking notes directly from the text. Whenever he encountered a subsequent passage that further stimulated his thinking
about a particular idea, he collated both passages on a fresh sheet
of paper in his notebook.[8] Besides taking notes, Napoleon
abstracted the history of ancient and modern governments and
the history of the Arabs, Hindus, Italians, English, and the
French. During the fateful year 1789, Napoleon continued to fill
his spare time by writing historical critiques. In retrospect, he
explained his motivation to Madame de Rémusat: "I studied
history less than I made a conquest of it; that is to say, I only
wanted and retained whatever could give me another idea, dis-
daining the useless and laying hold of certain results that pleased
me."[9]

Between 1797 and 1815, his years as an important public
figure, Napoleon on many occasions displayed the historical
nature of his thought. His correspondence reveals that he saw
himself foremost as a historical personage and that he held many
positive ideas about history. On one occasion, during the sum-
mer of 1802, Napoleon advised Jerome Bonaparte to live glori-
ously for the fatherland, because dying "without leaving any
trace of your existence, is not to have existed at all."[10] Not only
the intellectual milieu of his day, but perhaps also this consuming
sense of history led Napoleon to develop his ideas about the

nature and purpose of historical studies. Being a practical man, as well as a dreamer with a towering imagination, he made elaborate plans for the incorporation of history into the institutions and educational system of the First Empire, hoping thereby to inculcate young and old alike with his historicist philosophy.

Foremost among Napoleon's positive ideas about history was his certainty of the value of modern history. Because he was determined to direct all the arts toward subjects that would tend to enhance and to perpetuate the Empire, he was especially interested in contemporary history. He countered objections to his proposals to encourage the study of Imperial history by insisting that this would have enduring value. His opponents would be correct if history were satiric or panegyric, but the recitation of simple facts such as a call to arms, the making of a truce, or the sailing of a fleet was as true one year after the event as it would be a century later. To his opponents who maintained that only time permitted the formulation of judicious conclusions, Napoleon retorted that relating events while they were still fresh in all minds assured the veracity of material facts and permitted the instigation of useful debate as to the moral intention of those who made the decisions.[11]

While Napoleon appreciated historical accounts of periods, ancient history, for example, or the regional history of America, France, England, Germany, Italy, and Spain, he conceived very well the importance of specialized histories, particularly of law ranging from Roman times to the Consulate and of French military history. The content of the latter, he believed, should include the great campaigns of all times and the ways France's frontiers have been defended in various wars.[12]

Another indisputable point in Napoleon's view of history was his belief that historiography was already a science that merited further development. Claiming to be a great student of the muse, Napoleon said that he had wasted a great deal of valuable time reading poorly written history books because so many defective histories had been published. He was perturbed by the fact that "a man who wants to look for good instruction and who is suddenly placed in a vast historical library, finds himself in a real labyrinth." In fact, Napoleon thought so much history had been written that being able to discriminate among the original authors, good and bad commentators, and works well or mal-intended, was almost a science. To eliminate this confusion would be a real achievement, he argued.[13]

Napoleon was also emphatic in his belief that history is didactic. Military history, for example, is useful to the soldier who, warned of the errors of his predecessors, ought always to avoid committing the same errors; history contains equally precious lessons for statesmen. Since it rightly deals exclusively with facts, recent history could be especially useful to the military. The wars of the French Revolution could teach valuable lessons provided they were clearly perceived and transmitted.[14]

That the Emperor himself was increasingly attentive to the lessons of history is indicated by his choice of reading matter. In the Council of State on March 20, 1806, he remarked that he usually read medieval chronicles at bedtime; from these he learned that the Gauls were quite civilized until the barbarians brought them barbarism.[15] Two years later, in order to save space, he decided to have a portable collection of one thousand books printed without margins. He specified that he wanted about sixty histories included, and the bulk of the collection would be composed of historical memoirs written in every period. Among the histories, the Emperor wanted chronologies, works written by classical historians, and detailed histories of France. He also specified that Machiavelli, Montesquieu, and Voltaire should be included.[16] Over the years, moreover, Napoleon's interest in learning from history increased until in 1812 he had the novels and poetical works in his campaign library replaced by books of history.[17]

In addition, Napoleon maintained a constant interest in recently published works. He watched over the augmentation of the collections of the Bibliothèque Imperiale and planned to have it contain a copy of every good book existing in France. For the purpose of acquiring good French works that had been published since 1785 he allocated special funds.[18] Although Napoleon liked to read for pleasure, his more practical motives are discernible in the series of letters sent to his minister of police and to his librarian, Barbier,[19] between 1810 and 1812. Initially, the Emperor said he wanted to ascertain important information from all the books being printed in London.[20] In February, 1811, Napoleon wished to read all the works written by English officers on the last four campaigns of the Austrians and Russians.[21] The following month it was Abbé Fleury's book containing a detailed description of the Pragmatic Sanction of Bourges under the reign of Charles VII that he demanded.[22] In December, 1811, Napoleon informed himself with some "useful" documentation on Lithuania and Russia and asked for a bibliography of detailed French works on military operations and the campaigns of Charles XII in Poland and Russia.[23] A few weeks later it was historical materials on Courland, Riga, and Livonia that interested him.[24] At the same time, he had books in foreign languages translated if they had appeared abroad and were on the history of Russia. Hence, Méneval's[25] note to Barbier of May 7, 1812, ordered the librarian to send posthaste the translation made the previous winter of the English Colonel Wilson's work on the Russian army.[26] Even at Moscow Napoleon continued to follow what came off the presses.[27]

The importance Napoleon attached to documentation all his life guided his conduct at Malmaison on June 25, 1815, after his second abdication. When Napoleon prepared his library shipment by an American firm, he directed Barbier to bring him some works on America and a bibliography of works on his campaigns.[28] If the fallen Emperor behaved consistently, it may be conjectured from his choice of books at that time exactly where he planned to go and how he expected to engage himself with history once he arrived.

However Napoleon evaluated the different kinds of history, he insisted that the contents be useful facts presented clearly and simply, thereby making the presentation of historical facts coincide with the increasing efficiency, order, and martial quality of his own life and that of Imperial France. Besides these indisputable points, however, several ideas in Napoleon's statements about history are contradictory. For instance, he claimed to

accept the popular idea that "a historian is a judge who ought to
be the voice of posterity"[29] but, at the same time, he insisted that
historians should be chroniclers who record only facts, thereby
leaving the interpretation of history to the reader. Futhermore,
Napoleon stressed the idea that Imperial historians should be
talented enough to be both perfectly impartial and "right thinking" simultaneously. Once he mentioned to his ministers that so
many qualities are demanded of the model historian that he
found it difficult to believe that one could command a good history to be written and expect the order to be carried out.[30] Nevertheless, he instructed them to watch for "authors with real talent,
but still . . . loyal men, who present the facts from the true
perspective, and who prepare a sound education." Later he rei-
terated that the fundamental question to consider regarding the
hiring of an author is "whether he has the talent necessary,
whether he has a good mind, and whether one can count on the
sentiments which would guide his research and conduct his
pen." Such special characteristics were necessary even for the
men who merely wrote the continuations of existing textbooks
because "youngsters can only judge facts from the manner in
which they are presented. To mislead them in recounting remem-
brances, is to prepare them for errors in the future."[31]

Other ideas the Emperor adhered to are also hard to reconcile—history as a science and history as the servant of the
present. That Napoleon sometimes strongly favored the latter
view is apparent in the way he capitalized on the romantic spirit
of the times by weaving the rich historical heritage of the French
into the fibers of Imperial institutions. An interesting assortment
of historical figures appears in the *Correspondance* concerning
cultural affairs, public festivals, and the erection of monuments;
if the Emperor did not endorse an historical personage as suitable
for public emulation, it was because he judged him or her as being unworthy of a place in the memory of his loyal subjects. One
historical personage who seems to have figured very importantly
in the minds of both the Emperor and his close associates was
Charlemagne. For this reason Napoleon's identification with the
great Holy Roman emperor deserves special mention.

Napoleon clearly flirted with the idea of recreating Charlemagne's empire; his ministers wrote competing policy papers for him, outlining the ways he could recapture and surpass the greatness of the medieval Empire. In 1803, Napoleon started the bureaucratic wheels turning by ordering the erection of a statue of Charlemagne on either the Place de la Concorde or Place Vendôme.[32] Napoleon's coronation the following year was designed to make the public identify the new Emperor in their midst with his Frankish predecessor. Subsequently, Napoleon also became King of Italy. In 1806, Napoleon ordered the statue of Charlemagne that he had originally commissioned for the top of the Vendôme column sent to Aix-la-Chapelle. Less than a month later he formally acquiesced to Champagny's[33] petition that his own statue replace Charlemagne's atop the impressive monument. Champagny's request was suitably rhetorical: "What other statue could occupy the place which Charlemagne's leaves vacant?"[34] The chain of events surrounding the Charlemagne theme reveals how Napoleon's conscious ideas about his own and Charlemagne's significance in history changed at the beginning of the Empire: the heir of Charlemagne figuratively outshone even that august ruler.

Napoleon insisted upon having his identification with Charlemagne accepted beyond the borders of France. Between 1806 and 1809 he made several references to it in his dealings with the papacy. During these years Napoleon was very irritated with the Roman pontiff. He did not hesitate to tell His Holiness so, when the latter kept foreigners in Rome against Napoleon's wishes: "I am Charlemagne, the sword of the Church; I ought to be treated as such." After vituperating, he threatened the intransigent pontiff: "I am making known to the Pope my intentions in a nutshell. If he does not acquiesce to them, I will reduce him to the same condition where he was before Charlemagne."[35] In this instance Napoleon raised the dead to return the papacy to the position of vassalage it had occupied before Charlemagne gave it special status.

Napoleon's identification with Charlemagne continued to be a convenient political expedient as he extended his hegemony

over a great part of Europe.[36] In another letter to Talleyrand,
Napoleon pointed out to the minister of foreign affairs that when
he mounted the throne he assumed more than the rights of the
Bourbons, whose hegemony in Europe was incomparable to his
own. Rather, he assumed the rights of the Holy Roman emperors
and accordingly, relations with the papacy should be adjusted to
suit the historical situations as he interpreted them.[37] Napoleon
even urged his agent, Prince Eugène, viceroy of the Kingdom of
Italy, to exploit this historical fact; and in counseling the prince
about the phrasing of letters to the pope, Napoleon instructed his
protégé to make it clear to the pontiff that he was not speaking for
Louis the Debonair but, in effect, for Charlemagne.[38] By 1809
Napoleon decided to revoke the pope's temporal authority. He
justified his legal right to do this by asserting that the Donation of
Charlemagne only gave the bishops of Rome titles to fiefs that
maintained them as part of the Empire.[39] In the circular Napoleon sent to the bishops confirming his decision, he explained
that he was acting in the best interests of the people and of the
Christian religion by making Rome adhere to the original intentions of Jesus Christ.[40] As Napoleon evoked the past to sanction
his plans to recreate Charlemagne's Empire and to glorify himself, he audaciously pretended to be acting for the benefit of
religion and to do just what Jesus would do.

Napoleon's ministers recognized his obsession with Charlemagne and occasionally used this knowledge to flatter him. One
such occasion arose in a speech subsequently printed in the
Moniteur, when the crafty grand master of the Imperial University pointed out that while the French used to say that Charlemagne was the father of the university, they now proudly attributed this honor to the Emperor Napoleon.[41] Unquestionably,
by 1809 Napoleon eclipsed Charlemagne both in his own mind
and in the propaganda his minsters disseminated for public con-
sumption.

Charlemagne was not the only historical personage whom
Napoleon tried to revive. He also mentioned some famous women
in his *Correspondance*. In 1803 the Emperor expressed his admiration for Joan of Arc and the lesson that he learned from her life:

that the French national genius has always produced a suitable leader whenever its independence has been menaced by neighbors eager to profit from its internal disharmony.[42] In 1806, Napoleon put his stamp of approval on another medieval heroine, Jeanne Hachette, when he granted the petition of Beauvais to reestablish a traditional procession. On August 9, 1472, Louis XI had honored Jeanne and the women of Beauvais for their courageous conduct during a seige by Charles the Bold.[43] Because of their heroic conduct in defending the fatherland, unity, and national independence Napoleon enhanced the status of these fifteenth–century women in the Imperial interpretation of history, trying thereby to gain female support for his own policies by stressing the value of the personal sacrifices of their predecessors and identifying these popular figures with his regime.

Not all the famous women of history, however, received Napoleon's nod of approval. His cunning yet prudish sense of morality manifested itself when he ordered Cretet, his minister of the interior, to prevent the city of Troyes from erecting a monument to Agnes Sorel. In Napoleon's mind there was no reason to remember and honor a doubly tainted woman who was a king's mistress as well as a poetess.[44] Such an expression of disapproval disparaged the monarchy and served as a warning to the aspiring Agnes Sorels of the Empire, lest they too be eradicated from living memory by the Emperor in whose mind such a fate would be worse than death.

In addition to Napoleon's attempts to use the past to serve the present there is another flaw in his historical consciousness. Running through some of his letters there is an antihistorical tendency that is somewhat difficult to pinpoint, namely, the Emperor frequently merged the past and the present into an inseparable whole. Napoleon's identification with Charlemagne is a case in point.[45] It seems, setting his motives aside, that at times Napoleon imagined he actually was Charlemagne. On one occasion Napoleon wrote to his brother Louis, king of Holland: "You should understand that I do not separate myself from my predecessors and that, from Clovis to the Committee of Public Safety, I stand bound up with all of them"[46] This quality that characterizes some of Napoleon's writing was also noticed by one of his notorious enemies—Madame de Staël. She made at least a partially valid observation when she said tartly: "Respect for history is unknown to this man who conceives of the world only as being contemporaneous with himself."[47] Napoleon's inability to see the past except in relation to himself reveals an attitude that is irreconcilable with a true appreciation of history for its own sake.

A final aspect of Napoleon's historical policies helps to resolve some of the ambiguities in his idea of history. The tireless Emperor allocated time in his busy schedule to provide guidance for aspiring Imperial historians; in 1808, he went to great lengths to provide his subjects with appropriately written histories of France because he believed that no work was more deserving of his patronage. He carefully instructed these historians to write critically but not without bias about the past. The effects of ultramontanism should be felt in every line to arouse the French against foreign priests whose ambition might be to destroy the repose of Imperial France. Louis XIV had done some foolish things—such as revoking the Edict of Nantes and marrying the ridiculous Madame de Maintenon. The weaknesses that toppled the Valois and the Bourbons should be described so that people could better appreciate the accomplishments of the current regime. In short, "One ought to be just towards Henri IV, Louis XIII, Louis XIV, Louis XV, but without being adulatory."[48] When Napoleon was searching for the writers who would continue old classics such as Velly's *Histoire de France* and Président Hénault's *Abrégé chronologique*, he said: "They will divine easily, that my secret thought is to join together men who continue not philosophical history, not religious history, but the history of facts."[49] In short, Imperial historians did not suffer from lack of overall guidance aimed at making them better servants of the state.

Once the second abdication forced Napoleon's retirement from affairs of state, he resumed his historical work and this time it was with a mission. "If I have agreed to survive," he had orated to his Old Guard at Fontainebleau, "it is in order to serve your glory: I want to write down the great things we have done together." To write and to create history seemed entirely natural to him in order to make a place for himself in the memory of the people who gave his life true dimensions. On Saint Helena, with ample time for reflection, Napoleon devoted himself to this task, as much to escape boredom as to attract the favor of posterity.[50]

The fallen Emperor organized the composition of his historical work as he would a military campaign. He assigned specific jobs to each member of his entourage according to his aptitude. For example, Las Cases was assigned to the Italian campaigns, Bertrand handled the Egyptian campaign, while Gourgaud was given the Consulate and the Hundred Days. Even young Emmanuel Las Cases was not omitted—he was assigned to organizing the materials relating to the coronation era. Napoleon promised each of his companions that once the histories were dictated, corrected, and completed, he would not take credit for the authroship.[51]

Napoleon wrote most of his historical works about important events that had occurred since the Directory; this, of course, meant that much of his work was about himself and the military history of the Empire. In the few pieces that were not about recent history, the subjects were still military in nature; for example, the précis of the wars of Julius Caesar, Marshal Turenne, and Frederick the Great.[52] Napoleon always wrote in the vivid and concise style that characterized his correspondence. Many of his works are merely notes, critical observations, or explanations of the moral intent that underlay events. Sometimes, he wrote a narrative first and then annotated it—something he had done in his youth while reading the works of others.

In order to write his histories accurately, Napoleon first assembled the relevant documents. He used the *Moniteur* for reports, decrees, and official letters. On one occasion he ordered Gourgaud to prepare maps of Russia for use with the materials on the campaign of 1812. Articles in English were translated into French before Napoleon used them. When he worked on the campaigns of Julius Caesar, he used the *Commentaries* as a guide. With such documentation at hand, Napoleon dictated the history, which his companions wrote down.[53]

Despite his careful assembling of documentary evidence, the

literature Napoleon produced in exile is not a body of disinterested works. At Saint Helena, the fire of action past, he remained faithful to himself by trying to redeem from history the true meaning of his reign. In November, 1816. Napoleon told Las Cases that he wished more than fame and affection: he was pursuing immortality. The ultimate result of Napoleon's autobiographical works was the creation of the legend that became an important political factor during the larger part of the nineteenth century.[54]

In addition to writing history, Napoleon discussed it a great deal, thereby leaving some idea of his interpretation of the careers of several great historical figures. Among the ancients were Julius Caesar and Alexander the Great. Napoleon admired Alexander, who like himself was a youthful hero, warrior, and law-giver, but he noted that success corrupted Alexander: "He started out with the soul of Trajan; he ended up with the heart of Nero and the morals of Heliogabalus." In another conversation on Saint Helena the Emperor admitted that he could not understand Alexander's campaigns but he admired his political genius for winning the love of the people he conquered. Napoleon also identified his own career with that of Caesar, whose power was likewise legitimate because it was based upon popular will.[55]

Napoleon also discussed the kings of France, whom he generally did not hold in high regard. In a conversation in 1816, he commented that "Francis I was, after all, a mere hero of tournaments, a drawing-room beau, one of those monumental pygmies." As for the green gallant, "Henry IV never did anything great; he used to give 1,500 francs to his mistresses. Saint Louis was an imbecile. Louis XIV was the only king of France worthy of that name." Napoleon explained how it was that the French still idolized Henry IV: "Henry IV was a good man, but he accomplished nothing out of the ordinary; and when that gray-beard ran after the wenches in the streets of Paris, he was just an old fool. But in order to have a foil to Louis XIV, who was hated, he was praised to the skies." Napoleon's praise of Louis XIV, however, was mingled with criticism. Once he pessimistically remarked: "If Louis XIV had not been born king, he would have been a great man. But he did not know men—he could not know them. And besides, he never suffered ill fortune!" Napoleon's ambivalence showed itself again when he pointed out that the revocation of the Edict of Nantes, the dragonnades, the bull *Unigenitus*, and the treasury deficit were spots on the Sun King's image. Nevertheless, he allowed that Louis XIV was the only French king comparable to Charlemagne.[56]

The French Revolution inevitably entered Napoleon's conversations. Earlier, when he had stood in front of Rousseau's tomb at Ermonville, he opined that Jean-Jacques had prepared the Revolution but in 1816 he was struck with a somewhat unorthodox idea—that there had never really been a French Revolution because "the men of 1789 were the same as the men of Louis XIV's time."[57] Then he facetiously remarked that the manner in which the French people were able to swiftly change their allegiance can be attributed to their penchant for being fashionable. This was not, however, the interpretation he dictated for posterity, although his appreciation of historical continuity remained evident. Instead, he described the Revolution as a movement of the masses against the privileged classes whose feudal prerogatives exempted them from sharing the burden of taxation. The Revolution established equality of opportunity among the people, thus opening careers to talent and chance. The disparate regional elements were transmuted into a unified nation until, by 1800, France had been changed in accordance with "the well-being of the nation, with its laws, with justice, and with the spirit of the century."[58]

From dictating the history of the Revolution, Napoleon turned to predict that the revolutionary principles would forever be inextricably linked with the splendor of the Imperial era. "They live on in England, they illumine America, they are naturalized in France: from this tripod the light will burst upon the world." Besides being convinced that the revolutionary ideas would eventually become the established morality in the world, Napoleon was sure of his own place in history: "This memorable era will be linked to my person, because, after all, I have carried its torch and consecrated its principles, and because persecution now has made me its Messiah."[59] All of these remarks from Napoleon's conversations about great historical figures and events illustrate how his mind worked, imaginatively weaving his own experiences and achievements into the facts, whether remote or recent, to produce a peculiarly personal sort of history. They also show his tendency to engage in historical speculation.

The other marked aspect of Napoleon's historical thought during this final period of his life was his admitted Pyrrhonism. Then at leisure, he resumed the eternal debate over the objectivity of history, which he had tended to discount during the Imperial decade because of the overriding political considerations of establishing a state educational system to perpetuate his dynasty. He elaborated at length his ideas about historical truth:

> It must be admitted that the *true truths* are very difficult to ascertain in history. Fortunately they have more curiosity interest than real importance. There are so many truths! . . .
>
> Historical fact, which is so often invoked, to which everyone so readily appeals, is often a mere word: it cannot be ascertained when events actually occur, in the heat of contrary passions; and, if, later on, there is a consensus, this is only because there is no one left to contradict. But if this is so, what is historical truth in nearly every case? An agreed–upon fiction, as has been most ingeniously said.
>
> In all such things there are two very distinct essential elements—material fact and moral intent. Material facts, one should think, ought to be incontrovertible; and yet, go and see if any two accounts agree. There are facts that remain in eternal litigation. As for moral intent, how is one to find his way, supposing even that the narrators are in good faith? And what if they are prompted by bad faith, self-interest, and bias? Suppose I have given an order: Who can read the bottom of my thought, my true intention? And yet everybody will take hold of that order, measure it by his own yardstick, make it bend to conform to his plans, his individual way of thinking. . . . And everybody will be so confident of his own version! The lesser mortals will hear of it from privileged mouths, and they will be so confident in turn! Then the flood of memoirs, diaries, anecdotes, drawing–room reminiscences! And yet, my friend, that is history![60]

From this description of Napoleon's preoccupation with history during the three major periods of his life, several points become clear. He had a constant desire to master history and a sense of being a man of historical destiny. His desire to shape historical accounts and teaching to his will for the purpose of mastering people was actualized in various ways during his years in power and made his years of exile purposeful. His lapses into historical skepticism did not deter his overwhelming drive for the mastery of history, which he articulated to Madame de Rému-sat while he was enjoying the heights of popularity. At Saint Helena, that ambition was accomplished and fulfilled in the legend of his own creation. Aside from these psychological aspects of Napoleon's devotion to history, several definitely positive ideas emerge—his genuine interest in history, his appetite for facts, his philosophical historicism and his desire to make historical methodology more scientific. Moreover, his convictions about the didactic usefulness of history received practical application in the Imperial educational system.

History and the Imperial School Curriculum

We have seen that Napoleon had a pragmatic conception of history, that he had imaginative ideas about how it could be incorporated into the educational system to unify and solidify Imperial society. Moreover, it seems that by improving the quality of the teaching, reading, and writing of history Napoleon had the administrator's intention of simply making the educational system function more efficiently.

Public education was an institution born of the Revolution and pedagogy itself was in its infancy. Naturally, the concept of education for the masses, which was implicit in the egalitarian ideal, did not automatically become a reality with the demise of the Old Regime; it had to go through a transitional period. Moreover, the chaos of the Revolution was not especially conducive to establishing a public system of education, which lacked precedents. Knowledge about the history of French education in the first postrevolutionary decade is incomplete, but a grave picture of the conditions existing in education as the new century dawned is evident.

The system of public instruction created by the Convention consisted of two levels—primary schools and the *écoles centrales*. The course of study for the latter, which was prescribed by the law of 3 Brumaire, year IV (October 25, 1795), was divided into three grades for twelve-, fourteen-, and sixteen–year–old boys. The beginners studied drawing, natural history, and ancient languages and, in some departments, living languages as well. At the end of two years pupils were automatically promoted to the next class where they would study mathematics, physics, and chemistry. At age sixteen they passed into the third grade, where they concentrated on belles-lettres, history, legislation, and grammar. This curriculum lacked continuity, and the lax discipline then in force required neither mandatory participation nor any standard of achievement. With few exceptions the *écoles centrales* were unsuccessful. While theoretically history was emphasized more than during the Old Regime, actually little was taught. The professors were uncertain of both content and methods to follow; especially was this true of the law professors, whose occupation was becoming sterile.[1]

By 1801 nothing substantial had been done for primary education while the *écoles centrales*, established in the major city of each department, were dependent upon the primary schools to prepare their students. About two hundred schools of various kinds existed in the environs of Paris and as large a number in the provinces, but the quality of these institutions was mediocre. A crisis had developed, as two generations of children were completely illiterate.[2] A crisis existed not just because there were too few educational opportunities—these had never existed for the majority during the Old Regime and could not be missed—but because the Revolution had imbued citizens with the desire to be educated and to have their children educated. In short, there were too few good schools to meet public demand.[3]

Until the situation could be ameliorated, parents to whom primary schools were inaccessible had to undertake the elementary education of their children at home if they wished their boys later to be admitted to a secondary school or *lycée* or, in the case of most girls, to be educated at all. Obviously, parents or tutors needed textbooks; because of the ready market for sales, the publication of home instruction manuals proliferated during the Napoleonic era. Monthly literary reviews such as Michaud's *Journal général de la littérature de France* kept the public informed about the appearance of helpful books.[4]

In order to cope better with the educational crisis the consuls created a new administrative position in the government, that of director general of public instruction; the director's responsibility was to oversee all parts of public instruction—primary schools, the *écoles centrales* and collèges, *lycées*, *prytanées*, and other special boarding schools, theaters, and the Conservatoire

de Musique. Pierre–Louis Roederer,[5] a member of the Council
of State assigned to interior affairs, held this position briefly from
March until September, 1802.

Roederer kept well informed about the most recent educational theories and problems. Swiss friends recommended Pestalozzi's methods and reading textbook.[6] He considered the censorship problem; his solution was that while the police should
inspect all new publications and prevent the circulation of harm-
ful ones, authors who produced useful works should be rewarded
to encourage their zeal.[7] In addition, Roederer kept records of
which of the *écoles centrales* were suppressed.[8]

Roederer's papers reveal that he also considered at this time
remedying the deficiencies of the *écoles centrales* by replacing
seventeen of them in the major cities with *lycées* that would have
seven grades, to be financed by the money collected from the
octrois. The drafts of this project indicate the complete curriculum he envisioned. In the lowest grade, the seventh, boys would
study arithmetic, Latin, Greek, and French grammar. In the six
grade more complex arithmetic and decimals, general notions of
geography, cosmography, and history, French syntax, translation of French into Greek and Latin and vice-versa, grammatical
analysis of simple works in these three languages, and the ability
to teach the previous grade would be taught. The fifth grade
would consist of the development of cosmography, geography,
and history, more difficult Latin, Greek, and French, translation
of the easiest ancient history, better mastery of the teaching of
the two previous grades, in addition to studying civics (the duty
of teachers as loyal state servants). More arithmetic, notions of
chronology and ancient history, French, Greek, and Latin languages, harder translations of historians, and finally what Roederer called the duties of man and of the citizen, would be the fourth-
grade curriculum. In the next grade, elementary algebra, natural
history, economics (*économie animale*), notions of criticism and
history of the Middle Ages, the most difficult translations of historians, orators, and poets, French, Latin, and Greek prose composition and *réduction*, composition of Latin verse, and notions
of civil law would be studied. In the next–to–highest class, the

subjects would include elements of geometry, physics, and chemistry, analysis of *attendement*, modern history, speech, and writing in both prose and poetry. Finally, in the first class, algebra, geometry, physics and chemistry, logic, the history of France, geographical statistics, notions of public economy, and politics and diplomacy would be offered. In teaching all of these courses the professors would follow books lent to them by the government, and those teaching history or any other subject in the four upper grades would be specialists in their respective disciplines.[9]

Roederer's plan for revamping the curriculum of the *lycées* was not adopted; instead, the *corps législatif* approved the scheme presented by Minister of Public Instruction Chaptal on May 11, 1802, which was a more general plan.[10] Curiously, as the government orator for Chaptal's plan Roederer advocated a very different position from his personal views as described above. In fact, he spoke out strongly against teaching any subject, such as history specifically, that pupils could learn better on their own. Thus, for the sake of economy, he justified teaching a synthesis of social studies instead of the individual component disciplines. He stated emphatically that public instruction had for its immediate objective the distribution of useful and general information and not the advancement of knowledge.[11] This was not the only source of friction between Roederer and Chaptal; another sore point developed when Napoleon used the former as a check on the latter. In the autumn this uncomfortable triangular relationship ended with Roederer sharing the same fate as Fouché— demotion to senator, a position he held from September, 1802, until May, 1806.[12] Roederer's short term as director general of public instruction points up some of the issues being debated in 1802 about the schools and how deeply political intrigues, personalities, and financial problems were intertwined with the educational problems, which were far from being resolved. Although Roederer's ideas were not followed in 1802, some of them were put forth as Napoleon's own in the ensuing years and became a reality.

At the commencement of the Empire in 1804 educational practices still were not uniform or ideal and a conglomeration of schools existed. Some primary instruction was conducted on mother's knee, while private communal primary schools also helped to fill the need for elementary instruction. There were both communal and private schools on the secondary level, as well as the *écoles centrales*; the latter were still being phased out by the more advanced *lycées* and special schools. Some of the confusion resulted not only from the continued existence of schools with undefined or overlapping purposes but from the disappointing quality of educational legislation itself. But instead of a real solution, legislators improvised more detailed bureaucratic procedures for the system. An examination of this legislation indicates that teachers might accidentally be loyal servants of the state or good teachers but no one would have had a precise idea of what he should be doing, how he should do it, or why.

In his "Exposition of the state of the Republic" of January 16, 1804, Napoleon presented a glowing picture of education, noting that *lycées* and secondary schools were mushrooming all over France. The common rules, discipline, and uniform system of instruction in the *lycées* would instill virtues and talents in the younger generation, who would eventually bring glory to France. He singled out specific schools as evidence of the thriving educational system. The *prytanée* at Saint-Cyr, which educated the male orphans of citizens who died for the fatherland, inspired military enthusiasm. The special military school at Fontainebleau was noteworthy because it was producing hundreds of soldiers, and the interior of the vocational school at Compiegne looked like a factory with five hundred youngsters studying in the workshops.[13] Thus, Napoleon was proud of the fact that the schools were producing soldiers and tradesmen. In less public disclosures, however, Napoleon intimated his dissatisfaction with the actual state of affairs.

Napoleon's ideas about how to solve the educational crisis crystallized. In 1806, he created a government monopoly over education by establishing the Imperial University. In this way he hoped to develop and consolidate public spirit and thereby end the anarchic conditions in the Empire.[14] Another decree, issued in March, 1808, organized the administration of the Imperial

University in the form of the lay congregation. The Emperor would appoint a grand master as nominal head and through him he expected to have his ideas uniformly applied in all schools and, at the same time, to stifle private enterprise in education.[15] That Napoleon intended to maintain direct control over the educational system is corroborated by his comments made to the Council of State on May 21, 1806: "I am no longer affected by fear that a priest could one day be at the head of public instruction; with respect to that happening, what harm could it do since his agents would not be priests? This position of grand master will hardly be, as they imagine, second in the State."[16]

In February, 1805, Napoleon wrote a lengthy note on the reorganization of the *lycées*, commenting on the problem of staffing schools with good men at a price the Empire could afford; he said that perhaps it was time to consider forming an instructional order or teacher corps, using the Jesuit hierarchy as a model. Educators could be given *ésprit de corps* and motivation by starting as professors of the lowest grades and advancing, like their students, upward, a grade at a time, until they reached the top. After earning the highest teaching rank, a professor could become an administrator. Young men just starting their careers would remain celibate because they would not earn enough money to support a family. As they advanced in rank they would earn the privilege of marriage. By making their profession as prestigious as the Jesuits' had once been, Napoleon expected to compensate teachers for the years of self-denial.[17] Finally, in March, 1808, he issued the decree that was to make the teacher corps a reality. Nevertheless, even toward the end of the Empire staffing continued to be a problem as older professors died or asked to retire because of old age. To help with the teaching load *répétiteurs*, teaching assistants who merely reviewed the professors' lectures, had to be hired in many schools.[18]

In 1804, Napoleon finally admitted the necessity of providing public education for girls and instructed Cambacérès[19] and Portalis[20] to propose a "reasonable" solution.[21] In his "Exposition of the state of the Empire" of 1806, the Emperor reported that three houses of education had been established for girls because

the legislature, acting in its own self-interest, should not continue
to ignore the education of the sex that controlled the manners and
morals of the nation.[22] The curriculum Napoleon prescribed for
the girls' school at Écouen was quite simple; because these little
females in long-sleeved dresses were destined to become virtuous
wives and mothers, they were to study religion, French, and a
little geography and history, while the other three–fourths of
their time would be spent on handwork.[23] Napoleon seemed to
be thinking along the same lines then as when he decided in 1810
to educate only five thousand orphan girls: "What would they do
with this great number of girls when they reach twenty–one
years of age?"[24] Regardless of their destiny, learning a little history
would prepare females—whose most active passion he judged to
be vanity—for adulthood in Imperial France.[25]

Supplying cheap textbooks for the school system was another
problem that taxed the genius of Napoleon. Certainly by early
1805, the Emperor was aware that many people were complaining
about the cost of children's textbooks; he thought that "it would
be good to assign a commission to regulate the price of textbooks,
adopted by the *lycées*, at so much per sheet."[26] The heads of the
principal *lycées* of the Empire suggested another solution to this
grave and long–standing problem: provide the children with
specially collected anthologies containing lesson material, thereby
saving parents the expense of complete works. Such an anthology,
*Chefs-d'oeuvre d'éloquence tirées des oeuvres de Bossuet,
Fléchier, Fontenelle et Thomas*, appeared in 1806, and the
editor of this textbook declared that he had published it for this
reason. The text of this book also said that history could be studied
just as economically as other subjects by using official textbooks.[27] By making inexpensive textbooks available the government could more easily induce parents to buy them and teachers
to use them, thereby slanting the children's lessons automatically
to conform with official educational policies.

Napoleon was especially interested in the role of history in
the Imperial University. On April 2, 1807, the minister of interior
proposed that the Emperor establish four new chairs of history at
the Collège de France. He proposed one for the history of France,

and others for French eloquence, French poetry, and literary history and criticism. Napoleon's decision on this matter indicated his idea of the importance of these fields; he decreed instead the establishment of four chairs in French military history, the history of legislation in France, French eloquence and poetry, and literary history and criticism. Thus Napoleon tried to institutionalize his preference for the more practical fields of military and legal history.[28]

As an important part of the Imperial University Napoleon planned to establish a special school devoted to history. The plan for this had been incorporated into the law of 11 Floreal, year X (May 1, 1802) and Roederer, then director general of public instruction, made a notation on his copy that this was to be located in Paris;[29] however, it was not established then or after 1807. Nevertheless, the Emperor's plans for the school of history reveal a great deal about his views on history teaching in higher education. First of all, Napoleon argued that history deserved to be a special school because like geography it was one of the exact sciences that have something "really practical." The history department would be an information bureau of historical facts about Europe, Asia, Africa, and America, assembled, catalogued, and always including the latest information on current history. Moreover, "each of these professors would be, so to speak, a living book, and their courses would offer much of utility and interest to everyone having the desire or the need to be educated."[30] In addition, the school of history would teach its students bibliography and historical criticism. Another innovation he envisioned was to teach history that was not yet included in books because "no historian comes up to our time; there is always, for a man of twenty–five, an interval of fifty years which preceded his birth, on which there is no history."[31] Therefore, it would be the special obligation of the professors of the special school of history to fill the hiatus between where historians left off and the present moment.

More than a dozen chairs were provided for the proposed school of history.[32] There are two existing lists of these; one is Napoleon's, the other is that of the minister of the interior.

Napoleon listed separate chairs for Roman and Greek history; the
Bas-Empire; ecclesiastical history; American history; and several
others for the histories of France, England, Germany, Italy, and
Spain. After listing these posts Napoleon also stated his belief
that history should be divided according to the different purposes
for which it is taught; therefore, chairs for the history of legislation from the Romans to the Consulate and of French military art
would yield "very great advantages."[33] The minister of the interi-
or's list is similar, but its ten chairs are the following: literary
history and criticism, military history, religious history, legislation, ancient history, medieval history, French history, modern
northern Europe, modern southern Europe, and biography.[34]
The differences in the two lists again emphasize Napoleon's
tendency to downgrade literary subjects in education. Another
interesting difference is that Napoleon included chairs for English
and German history, indicating military and political motivations
on the Emperor's part.

Education at the superior level was discussed by the Council
of the Imperial University in February, 1810, and to create more
uniformity, special statutes were written specifying how history
would be taught by Facultés des Lettres et des Sciences. Initially,
each of the faculties created by the decree of March 17, 1808, was
to have three professors representing belles-lettres, philosophy,
and history. The history professor "will explain the principles of
chronology, the great epochs of history and the concordance of
ancient and modern geography." Each professor, however, would
be responsible for knowing the history of his own science, as well
as the names of the best authors and works in his field. Arrayed
in academic garb, professors at these institutions would teach
three ninety–minute lessons weekly, for nine months.[35]

Special statutes also established a more specialized curriculum
for the Faculté des Lettres et des Sciences de Paris. Courses
there would consist of two, ninety–minute lectures weekly, for
only eight months. Nine separate courses would be offered: Greek
literature, Latin eloquence, Latin poetry, French eloquence,
French poetry, philosophy, the history of philosophy, ancient
and modern history, and ancient and modern geography. The

duties of the history professor were to compare the important systems of chronology, to describe the manners and customs of civilizations, to trace the rise and fall of empires, and to establish and apply rules of historical criticism.[36]

During 1810 and 1811 the Council of the Imperial University also discussed the curriculum and methods for the proposed Ecole Normale, for which the council felt there was an urgent need. A team–teaching method was devised whereby professors would deliver lectures and *répetiteurs* would conduct compulsory seminar–like discussion sections to prepare students for the *baccalauréat*.[37] At these sessions students would analyze the writing of noted authors and read their own historical compositions and papers. After students had these lectures and seminars and had mastered the art of criticism, they would be ready for the capstone: actual practice teaching. As preparation they would study elementary textbooks and discuss the classroom presentation of material. These discussions would be followed by lesson simulations. Thus, students at the Ecole Normale would receive practical as well as theoretical training before they were eligible for appointments as teachers of history or other subjects in Imperial *lycées*.[38]

Napoleon was deeply disturbed by all the problems in education, many of which were financial in nature. In February, 1805, he wrote at length about how the *lycées* should be reorganized to put them on a paying basis, especially since they were costing more to operate per pupil than private institutions. To correct this the Emperor intended to audit each institution's accounts in order to determine the number of students each would require to operate at optimum efficiency. He also wondered whether there were too many administrators and professors in certain *lycées*. Moreover, he thought there were instances where professors of unequal merit were receiving the same salary. In addition to costing too much, the *lycées* were to Napoleon's way of thinking being run dangerously, as he verified on his personal inspection tour when he spied women inside the buildings.[39] The same solution to the problems of supplying textbooks, hiring qualified personnel, and running the entire school system always confronted

Napoleon: "money and always more money!"[40] As this obvious solution became more impossible, at the same time it became more imperative for the salvation of the Empire.

Another problem Napoleon had to deal with was the duplicity of some administrative and instructional personnel of the Imperial University. In addition to the attitude of the antigovernment priests, which might be expected under the circumstances, two important figures may be singled out among the opposition— Louis Fontanes and François Guizot.

As president of the *corps législatif* Fontanes had earned a sizable reputation for his speeches containing the basest flatteries of the Emperor.[41] However, in 1804, he had written about the juridical murder of the Duke of Enghien in an ode, voicing his opinion that the affair was a political and moral crime.[42] Once he became grand master of the Imperial University Fontanes continued to voice opposition to the Emperor's actions. His appointment itself marked the triumph of the Catholic party over the *philosophes*[43] and lends credence to the idea that Napoleon intended to reestablish the monarchy. Publicly Fontanes continued his flattery of Napoleon by calling him the new Charlemagne; nevertheless, after the decree of March, 1808, integrated the church schools and seminaries into the university monopoly, Fontanes exempted the small seminaries from compliance with the law. Fontanes also circumvented the emperor's intentions in another way: church schools were not inspected without the bishop's invitation or without prior warning of when the inspection would occur. Fontanes definitely tried to favor Catholic elements in defiance of the laws of the university.[44] This practice of favoritism eventually came to Napoleon's attention and was at the heart of the dispute between Fontanes and Montalivet,[45] the minister of the interior. Napoleon refused Fontanes' requests that he be granted equality with Montalivet and be removed from under his jurisdiction by reminding him that no one, including the prince imperial, could be the equal of one of his ministers.[46] In fact, in July, 1810, Napoleon used Montalivet to rebuke Fontanes for corresponding with bishops instead of the prefects and for making public instruction an affair of religion.[47]

Fontanes' administration of the university conflicted with Napoleon's views in another area. He did not share Napoleon's admiration for history; rather, Fontanes admired ancient education with its emphasis on literature. He tried to defend education against what he called "the passions of the times,"[48] that is, Napoleon's desires for the schools to produce soldiers instead of thinkers. This led Fontanes to attempt to institute from above an apparent regularity in the exercises while leaving the study of the textbooks more or less up to the individual instructor's discretion.[49] Fontanes apparently did not work too hard at making the schools conform; as he told one of his friends, he always spent four hours every day writing poetry before opening his desk and attending to affairs of state.[50]

Napoleon had too much at stake to permit a versifying social climber like Fontanes a free rein. Through his minister of police, Fouché (who happened to be a Freemason and avid atheist),[51] the Emperor countered Fontanes' actions. This aspect of Napoleon's program for incorporating history into the curriculum of Imperial schools reveals that Napoleon's ministers, sometimes, in addition to lacking character, worked at cross-purposes.[52]

Information about another of Napoleon's appointees, François Guizot, indicates that the spirit of Bonapartism did not always pervade the University of Paris. Guizot and his bride–to–be, Mlle. Pauline de Meulan, had requested permission from the Duc de Rovigo in February, 1811, to publish a monthly journal to help parents with their children's education. The minister conferred with the censor Esmenard, who assured him that since both of them were loyal and capable "the enlightened protection which your excellency accords to writers who are faithful to the Imperial dynasty and to public morality could not be better placed."[53] After receiving Imperial approval Guizot edited the *Annales d'Education* until 1814; the articles he wrote and published in it were quite innocuous. But in 1812, Fontanes divided the chair of history held by Lacretelle the Younger at the University of Paris and gave twenty–five–year old Guizot the position in modern history.[54] Through his contacts with the faculty Guizot became associated with the ideological opposition to which they belonged.[55] This intellectual elite was basically passive and apolitical, but the young professor, whose ideas were germinating, was more obstinate. When Guizot gave his inaugural address in December, 1812, he refused to follow Fontanes' polite suggestion that he include one or two laudatory remarks about the Empire. Moreover, from his chair he made allusions to the parallel between the despotism and conquering ambitions of the Romans and the deeds of Napoleon. In fact, the audacity of some of Guizot's remarks indicates that not only was there freedom of expression in the university, but outright vocal opposition to the basic purposes of the educational monopoly.[56]

In addition to the problems already described and an occasional student riot,[57] Napoleon faced another critical problem over which he had little or no control—time. His dream of creating uniformity of opinion among forty million Europeans was so ambitious that it was impossible to realize in the short time allotted to him. Napoleon made his own and best apology when he wrote from Saint-Helena: "I had asked for twenty years; destiny gave me only thirteen of them."[58] Moreover, during the truncated life span of the Empire Napoleon divided his time among all Imperial affairs. He simply could not occupy himself solely with any one aspect of governmental policy, especially when his presence was required on the battlefield. Such an impossible program involving inert institutions and a vast bureaucracy was bound to disappoint the Emperor's expectations for instant improvement and development. In spite of all the problems, however, the establishment of the Imperial University was a durable achievement.[59] For this reason, the success of Napoleon's efforts to have all the students in Imperial France study history deserves to be examined objectively.

All evidence indicates that Napoleon's vision of French education was often not translated into reality. The actual programs for teaching history above the *lycée* level in the Empire hardly resembled that envisioned by Napoleon. At the University of Paris there were two chairs of history and geography combined, one ancient and one modern. Each professor taught the chronologies of the great epochs of history and the comparative tables of the law, arts, and manners of these civilizations, in addition to establishing rules of criticism and applying them to other historians. This program resembled the Emperor's envisioned program in certain ways; however, it was impossible for one man to do the work of several.[60] Moreover, the curriculum was still classical and oriented toward letters, with emphasis placed on antiquity and the seventeenth century.[61] Except at the University of Paris the quality of instruction was mediocre. The *facultés des lettres* at Amiens, Besançon, Bourges, Caen, Cahors, Clermont, Dijon, Grenoble, Limoges, Lyon, Montpellier, Nancy, Nîmes, Orléans, Pau, Poitiers, Rennes, Rouen, Strasbourg, Toulouse, Brussels, Genoa, Geneva, Parma, and Turin all had chairs of history.[62] The *lycées*, however, were not, by the Emperor's own admission, doing the job they should have been,[63] and there history was hardly a uniform discipline.[64]

In order to learn how well his ideas about the teaching of history and the use of the official textbooks were enforced Napoleon sent a questionnaire to the prefects in 1811. Although no exact criteria for indicating conformity or nonconformity to the laws of the Imperial University were established, it is possible, by reading the prefects' responses, to discern how the government expected history to be taught.[65] A prefect's favorable report probably meant that the official textbooks were in use; ancient, medieval, and modern history were being taught; the Fourth Dynasty[66] was the subject of compositions; the teachers supported Napoleon wholeheartedly and drew laudatory analogies between ancient history and current events in order to glorify the Emperor; and the students were taught in every way possible to love His Majesty and France. One prefect noted that the Collège de Langres was one of the best academies; it had five hours of lessons daily with the first–year grammar class using textbooks on illustrious lives and sacred history, the second–year grammar class using Rollin's *abrégé* of ancient history, and the second–year humanities class using a textbook on the history of France.[67]

The reports that contain adequate information indicate that more departments conformed than failed to comply. However, the criticisms of the nonconforming schools varied. Some schools failed to receive official approval because they did not teach the history of the Fourth Dynasty;[68] in others contemporary history was taught, but it was over-shadowed by the great emphasis placed on ancient history.[69] In other departments, it was apparent in the way they taught history that the teachers seemed to be completely indifferent to the interests of the government.[70] These reports also indicated that nonconformity was not always caused simply by bureaucratic adherence to accustomed methods. In the case of the ecclesiastical schools the priests opposed the government for what they considered to be religious reasons. In a few cases, however, the prefects indicated that the teachers expressed their willingness to teach the history of the Fourth Dynasty as soon as they received the official textbooks.[71]

After Napoleon's abdication some educators still defended his educational endeavors. During the fifth month of the Bourbon Restoration a former inspector general of education of the Napoleonic era, Joseph Izarn, wrote a defense of the Imperial University in which he expressed conviction that students received a better education than formerly at the University of Paris. Moreover, he maintained that education had improved so much that instruction given in Imperial *lycées* equaled that formerly existing at the university level. Izarn also commented specifically on history teaching and how it had improved in a similar manner.[72] Thus, even when it was opportune to deny Bonapartist sentiments, at least one Imperial educator defended Napoleon's success with the history curriculum.

In conclusion, although the teaching of history in the Imperial University was not the great instrument of his reign that Napoleon hoped it would be, much progress was made. Since history never achieved the position Napoleon had envisoned for it in 1806, the world will never know if his political ideas about its importance in the curriculum were correct. Nevertheless, the Bourbons would have to do more to rid themselves of the ghost of Napoleon and the muse of history than replace the drummers in the schools by bells because the dozens of history textbooks that appeared actually institutionalized the kind of history that His Majesty ordered for years to come.

The Teaching of History in the Imperial Schools

Theoretically and from the standpoint of organization, Napoleon succeeded in making history a part of the curriculum of Imperial schools. Much can be learned about teaching methods and the actual contents of specific courses by examining some of the primary and secondary history textbooks that were published during the First Empire.

Scattered evidence exists to explain how history textbooks and methods were adopted by the government. Shortly after the basic legislation on education—the law of April 22, 1802—was enacted, a textbook commission was established to select official textbooks for teaching history in the secondary schools and *lycées*. By an act of May 15, 1803, the members of the commission— Fontanes, Champagny, and Domairon—adopted three books: Domairon's own *Rudiments d'histoire*, Sérieys' *Tablettes chronologiques à l'usage du Prytanée français . . .* , and a wall chart by Le Prévost d'Iray.[1] After this, however, no more is heard from this commission. That its function was sometimes assumed by the police is indicated by Fouché's reports to the Emperor.[2] In subsequent years many history textbooks for primary, secondary, military schools and the *lycées* were published; that they were somehow officially adopted is indicated in their complete titles or on their title pages.

After the creation of the Imperial University more care was taken to supervise the curriculum and to make textbooks uniform. When the College of St. Amand in the department of Cher was reorganized in 1809, its new regulations stipulated that "the books adopted for the classes of *lycées* will be the only ones put into the hands of the students of the college."[3] A regulation on instruction in *lycées*, which was also published in 1809, said that the two years of humanities would include lessons in history and they "would direct their readings in such manner as to give them the principal notions of history. There will be for this purpose, in the classrooms, geography maps and chronological tables." The regulation went on to stipulate that, in addition to Plutarch's *Lives*, textbooks on the revolutions of Rome, Sweden, and Portugal and Voltaire's history of Charles XII would be studied. Finally, beginning in 1815 no professor would be appointed to teach unless he had first passed the *agrégation*.[4]

In 1811 the responses of the prefects to Napoleon's questionnaire on education indicated that official and other textbooks on all subjects were in use in the Imperial University and that these contained ancient and modern history, including that of the Fourth Dynasty.[5] To enforce uniformity the Council of the Imperial University stipulated that official textbooks must be used for every subject in all schools and that a list of them would be drawn up annually for use the following year.[6]

The registers of the deliberations of the council of the Imperial University of 1813 make it clear that by that time the Council had assumed governmental responsibility for selecting and adopting official texts. First the "Commission des livres classiques" examined the books, and if it approved them, the "Section du perfectionnement des études" proposed their adoption in a report to the council. Many long sessions[7] were devoted to hearing and discussing such reports from the Section de l'Etat et du Perfectionnement des Etudes. Thus, for example, on July 13, 1813, Christophe-Guillaume Koch's *Tableaux des Révolutions de l'Europe*, which had been praised by the Institut in a report to the Emperor, was officially adopted for use in the libraries of *lycées* and the *école normale* and recommended to professors of history because it inspired "the love of the good, the just and the beautiful."[8] The following October these other histories were approved conditionally, while not prescribed as actual texts: Vertot's *Révolutions romaines* and Voltaire's *Histoire de Charles XII* and *Siècle de Louis XIV*.[9] By the end of the year the university had spent 3,000 francs on the acquisition of books on all subjects that it had approved for the schools.[10] Since all history textbooks were carefully censored or approved by official commissions in this way, they are a valid object of study for discerning Napoleon's policies about the teaching of history.

Napoleon mobilized the dead to produce history textbooks. The works of Président Hénault, Abbé Millot, Rollin, Bossuet, Abbé Le Ragois, Raynal, and Vertot reappeared. Occasionally they were reprinted intact, but usually they were adapted to suit a particular age level or continued to the date of re-publication by an Imperial historian.[11]

Other textbook writers were alive. Certainly one of the liveliest was Antoine Sérieys, an erstwhile professor of history with the reputation of a charlatan, who produced about a dozen history textbooks.[12] Another textbook writer, Le Prévost d'Iray, had been a viscount during the *ancien régime*. After he became impoverished, he made his living first by writing a number of comedies, then by teaching history, and later by becoming an *inspecteur général* of education.[13] Marie-Joseph Chénier was a playwright who had the misfortune of having his greatest tragedy proscribed by Napoleon. After working for a while as an archivist, he accepted a cash gratuity and a pension of 8,000 francs from the Emperor and set to work on a continuation of Abbé Millot's *Histoire de France* which Napoleon wanted written.[14] Louis Domairon, another textbook writer and inspector of public instruction, had served a novitiate as a Jesuit. Before the Revolution he taught literature at the Ecole Royal Militaire. After living obscurely during the Revolution he resumed his profession until he was named to the textbook commission.[15] Jean-Charles Lacretelle, called Lacretelle the Younger, won his early reputation as a publicist, but in 1809, Napoleon appointed him to the faculty of letters of Paris despite his known royalist sympathies.[16] This potpourri of textbook authors illustrates that Napoleon employed whatever men were ready, willing, and able to do the job according to specifications, even if their loyalty, ethics, and talent as historians were questionable.

The scope of Imperial history textbooks was broad. At the beginning of the Empire many books were published on ancient history. These usually included discussions of ancient methods of reckoning time, various systems of chronology, and both sacred and profane ancient history. Modern histories, that is, books on history since the fall of the Roman Empire in the West, emphasized the Middle Ages and barely outlined history since the death of Saint Louis. However, in the later years of Napoleon's Empire new, modern history textbooks shifted their emphasis so that more space was devoted to the history of the Bourbons, the French revolutionary period, and the Fourth Dynasty. Moreover, most new textbooks or new editions of previously published works were continued right up to the month of publication. Sometimes survey texts were even arranged so as to teach pupils modern history first.[17] The scope of Imperial history textbooks ranged from the creation of the world to the present, with increasing emphasis on the latter. Thus the teaching of history moved more in line with Napoleon's ideas and away from a condition that Napoleon criticized when he said, "All our young people find it easier to learn about the Punic Wars than to know about the American War, which occurred in 1783. . . ."[18]

The scope of Imperial history textbooks was also broad in the sense that they covered not just European but world history. This was true all during the Consulate and Empire. Sometimes, even textbooks that were called histories of France actually contained much more. For example, in Domairon's *Rudiments d'histoire* the volume on France also included the British Isles from the Anglo-Saxons to Richard Cromwell, a few pages on each area of Europe within the boundaries of the French Empire in 1804, as well as short histories of Prussia, Poland, Russia, Turkey, North Africa, Arabia, Tartary, India, China, and Japan, with special emphasis on the problems of Christianity in the last three countries.[19] Sometimes separate lessons were even given on Asiatic Russia after India, China, and Japan had been covered.[20] In 1804, Sérieys in his *Tablettes chronologiques à l'usage du Prytanée français*[21] placed even more emphasis on China and Egypt, and in the 1806 edition he added the history of Algeria.[22] The next year Sérieys published a textbook on the history of Portugal.[23] In 1807 a three–volume history of Germany to 1705 appeared.[24] The history of colonial America and the United States was given some sort of brief but romantic treatment in most textbooks.[25] Subsequent textbooks mentioned almost every area of the world except sub-Sahara Africa and South America. In sum, the scope of geographical areas included in Imperial history textbooks often paralleled Napoleon's military conquests, daydreams, or expressed interests.

History textbooks that were broad in scope were especially suitable for teaching students by what educators called the "synchronistic methods," that is by studying what was happening simultaneously in several countries. In the officially sanctioned journal of education François Guizot stated that this technique was valuable because it joins facts together "following the historical sciences" and "engraves dates in the memory while attaching them to each one of the facts belonging to the same epoch."[26] The synchronistic method could be adapted to suit various instructional materials.

Several kinds of formats were used for Imperial history textbooks, and in some cases the format dictates that a specific instructional technique be used by the teacher. On the whole, history texts were either wall charts, chronologies, catechisms, poetry, or various combinations of these schemes. Authors tried to avoid writing simply narrative histories. They also competed with each other in creating books that suited the needs of both pupils and teachers while exemplifying the most up–to–date psychological theories about the learning process. From an examination of these formats it becomes apparent that in the schools children were expected to do more than read a textbook and listen to a lecture in order to know history.

The textbooks adopted during the first years of the Empire were chronologies, a format that continued to appear later. Some of the shorter chronologies were published in two different folio editions: in the usual paginated form and on fold-out sheets of paper so that they could be hung on the schoolroom wall. A typical wall chart for use in *lycées* contained parallel columns for individual countries of Europe, Asia, North Africa, and America.[27] The entries on these charts were so brief and factual, however, that they left a great deal to the instructor's discretion. If he wished he could give different interpretations or explanations of the causes of the events without contradicting the printed material that the pupils memorized and used as a basis for compositions. On the other hand, even if a teacher wanted to bolster the Napoleonic regime, there was no way that he could be sure of giving the "best" interpretation of history when the inspectors visited his classes or at any other time. We have seen that Napoleon defined a good historian as "a judge who ought to be the voice of posterity."[28] If an Imperial history teacher made an error of judgment, however, he might incur the wrath of the emperor who complained repeatedly: "Good Lord! How stupid these men of letters are!"[29] Lack of guidance possibly created a dilemna for the instructor who used chronologies.

Another type of format—the history catechism—became increasingly popular during the Empire. Sometimes the entire textbook was organized into short lessons so as not to fatigue the youngsters. For younger children each lesson consisted of a short narrative of events, followed by a series of questions and answers taken verbatim from the preceding pages. Catechisms for older pupils had longer answers that could be memorized only by well–developed minds.[30]

One author, Girard de Propiac, who was archivist of the Seine, wrote three of these catechisms. His first one, which appeared in 1804, was a small two–volume abridgment of Plutarch's *Lives* designed for boys and girls.[31] Two years later he published expressly for girls an adaptation consisting of the lives of famous women in history. Incidentally, Propiac explained that he wrote this one because so much care was being taken with female education, and that with proper training women, who in the past were subjugated by the jealousy of men, could equal their courage, virtue, and heroism.[32] But Propiac did not merely employ the question–and–answer format for histories of the classical era; he also wrote a catechism for both boys and girls on the history of France from the origin of the Franks to July, 1807.[33]

Abbé Gaultier, another author who wrote a history catechism,[34] deserves special mention. Gaultier was a noted educator who wrote a complete course of studies for primary education that included textbooks on reading, writing, arithmetic, the French laguage, Latin, Italian, geography, and the art of thinking, as well as on chronology and history.[35] Gaultier's method for helping children memorize ancient and modern history is note-worthy: he composed historical data into verse that he used along with questions and answers. Gaultier maintained that children not only could learn these little rhymes more quickly than dull chronologies, they could also remember them all their lives; in fact, the poems would make learning history fun.[36] The questions and answers the children memorized explained and interpreted the contents of the verses; thus each process reinforced the other. Gaultier made an effort to incorporate into his book Buffon's knowledge of the use of sensory perception in learning. In addition to the verses and catechism he included a set of thirty–two flash cards, which were done in three colors to correspond to the three great divisions of history. The children or the teacher could hold these to expedite the memorization of the lesson and make learning even more enjoyable. The card representing church history from 1801 to 1807 contained these four lines:

> Le pontife à Paris sacre Napoléon,
> D'après les divins rites de la Religion.
>
> Il gagne tous les coeurs et relève la croix.
> Le fidèle à genoux se soumet à sa voix.[37]

Gaultier had not exhausted his ideas yet, however; he incorporated the technique of mutual education[38] into his book by arranging the table of contents so that teachers could use it to teach grammar along with history.[39] In all of these ways Gaultier tried to help children develop memory banks like those of elephants.[40]

The point that many of the Imperial history textbooks were catechisms need not be belabored, but the appearance of this particular format has important implications. It was certainly a boon to history teachers. Catechisms enabled them to use class time more efficiently and, by providing ready-made lessons, freed the teachers for other duties. Moreover, there was no need for the most timid teachers to fear giving an incorrect interpretation of history because the correct interpretation was already supplied. The appearance of catechisms themselves implied that the teaching of history was moving away from the teaching of simple facts and dates to the teaching of an official interpretation of events. In fact, with the use of catechisms there no longer was any need for history teachers to know any history—a practical way to overcome the shortage of trained teachers. Teachers who really loved their pupils could apply the rote method to teaching history and, at the same time, follow Pestalozzi's method of mutual education.[41]

Although history was a serious and important subject, Imperial educators often placed great emphasis on making it fun for children to learn by turning it into forms of amusement such as playing cards, games of make-believe, and entertaining stories like Fréville's two–volume *Histoire des chiens célèbres . . .,*[42] which could be used to fill idle hours more beneficially and to stimulate interest in learning. Two examples of historical games also provide insight into the psychological assumptions behind the creation of such amusements. *The Jeux de cartes historiques, contenant l'Histoire Sainte, depuis la création du monde jusqu'à la naissance du Messie . . .* was designed for use by both girls and boys. The children were supposed to study the picture and historical précis on each card, and "in this manner, facts and names would be engraved in their memory, the only faculty of their understanding that can be trained in them yet."[43] The "Academy of Sciences" game, in which children pretended they were academicians who displayed their vast knowledge of history, geography, mathematics, and other fields to a king whose intelligence might be quite inferior, taught children about the functioning of learned societies similar to the Institut de France. Contemporary educational psychology involving emulation, praise, and ridicule was incorporated into the rules of the game. As its designer pointed out, rural youngsters could occupy themselves after supper or on rainy days, and concomitantly ward off slothfulness, by doing such delightful domestic chores as shelling peas or peeling fruit, but little city-dwellers faced the danger of being bored from idleness.[44] Although games requiring some historical knowledge had been used in the Little Schools of Port-Royal, they were now considered even more useful in an urban locale.

The general guidelines Napoleon established for the censorship of all books[45] also applied to history textbooks, but certain definite trends are noticeable in the subject matter of Imperial history textbooks published over the years. There was a general trend toward teaching modern history, including the period in French history from Saint Louis to Louis XVI. Moreover, modern history and especially contemporary history were presented as being more important and more glorious than the history of antiquity. Certain specific themes showed a more rapid and decided development of bias in their content.

Even the study of ancient history was written in a contemporary vein and many of the details considered important enough to include in the accounts were related to recent events in France. For example, in discussing the assassination of Julius Caesar, Marie François Desormes singled out one notable accomplishment—that after terminating the civil wars, Caesar reformed the confusion in the calendar. Brutus was described as a fanatical republican who killed a great man, thereby plunging the country into misfortune. The Romans "needed a master. And who was more worthy to be master than Caesar? And who could replace this great man?"[46] And who was the only person the pupils knew who could be the new Caesar; who was it who had straightened out the confusion in their own republican calendar? The suggested response was so obvious they could have answered in unison—"The Emperor Napoleon."

Another subject, the history of the Gauls, was an appropriate one for pupils to study at a time when France had regained her ancient limits. Sérieys published two textbooks on this subject that put forward definite interpretations about their high degree of civilization. In his earlier book, he said that kings had existed in Gaul for a long time before Caesar conquered it and even before Rome was built.[47] In a later book, Sérieys described land tenure in ancient Gaul in order to show that Charlemagne's conquest made the title of Holy Roman Emperor rightfully hereditary in the Carolingian family for the same reason.[48] The French monarchy, as every child knew, was established by Pharamond in the year 420:

> Ce prince, des Français fut le premier des rois;
> Et le premier aussi qui leur donna des loix.[49]

Hence, Clovis was the fourth French king and Charlemagne the twenty–fourth, of whom one textbook said:

> Au milieu des combats je n'eus point de pareil
> Je fus plus grand encore en prudence, en conseil.[50]

Another author painted Charlemagne in prose: "Here unquestionably is the greatest of our kings, the one who did the most, and who, by the power of his genius alone, raised himself so far above his century that he still appears today as a colossus."[51] The textbook written by a member of the Institut mentioned that when Charlemagne died he left an article in his capitularies allowing for the nation to decide which of his three sons should succeed him as emperor because he recognized the people's right to choose their sovereign.[52] This sort of treatment of medieval kingship reinforced contemporary ideas of nationalism and the sovereignty of the people.

The Bourbons were treated well in Imperial history textbooks. While most of them told about Henry IV's putting a chicken in every peasant's pot, one 1805 textbook for the *lycées* contained a description, several pages in length, of Henry IV's plan for a European army and government to perpetuate peace;[53] in fact, according to Mentelle's history course, Henry IV was occupied with his plan to pacify all of Europe when he was assassinated.[54] Along with all of his great qualities children were also apprised of Henry IV's faults, especially that "he was too fond of gambling and women."[55]

During the Consulate, the reigns of the Bourbon monarchs who followed Henry IV were severely criticized for the manner in which the wars used up men and money, in addition to the fact that the "nation" became as impotent as the monarchy became powerful.[56] However, later authors of adopted texts interpreted

Louis XIV as ambivalently as Napoleon did. As students of the Prytanée Français learned, Louis XIV earned the title of Louis the Great because he typified the genius and good taste of the best rulers of Greece and Rome, but his excessive expenditures and wars drained the realm.[57] Certainly, Louis XIV's magnificence was somewhat eclipsed by the equally or more effusive treatment allotted by most authors to his royal successors.

An 1810 textbook pointed out that Louis XV's reign was great because he encouraged astronomy, navigation, mathematics, technology, and agriculture; and he established the Ecole Militaire and the Ecole de Chirurgie.[58] Girard de Propiac facilitated memorization by summing up Louis XV's reign poetically:

Louis le Bien-Aimé, souverain de l'enfance,
Admiré de l'Europe et chéri de la France;
Père de ses sujets, dont il fut adoré,
Devint l'honneur du trône et de l'humanité;
et sûr, en combattant, d'enchaîner la victoire,
Il chercha dans la paix une plus juste gloire.
On ressentit l'effet de ses soins généreux,
et sous un tel, monarque on ne put qu'être heureux.[59]

The reign of Louis XVI, however, received the most interesting treatment allotted to the Bourbons. Writers in the first years of the Empire seem to be wary of Louis XVI. Most early chronologies simply included a line or two about his reign and the fact that he died. About 1808, however, Imperial textbooks began to revive Louis XVI, and he was praised for everything except his lack of enough courage to please the French.[60] Also, in that year the regicides were presented as "butchers" and "monsters."[61] By 1810 Louis XVI was viewed as the good, kindly, humane, thrifty king whose reign destroyed the remnants of feudalism. The American Revolution opened the door to Louis XVI's misfortunes and finally led him to the scaffold.[62] The Louis XVI whom pupils at the Ecole Militaire studied was the good king whose experience proved that too much goodness and indulgence are fatal qualities in a ruler;[63] moreover, the touching details of his final hours were now included.[64] He was still assessed as having only one flaw—

lack of courage, but now the Parisians were horrified by the bloody
sacrifice of their king, which their own feebleness permitted the
"monsters" to perform. The Parisians had expiated their errors
by suffering through the misfortunes they thus brought upon
themselves and endured until a powerful hand miraculously
delivered them.[65] The poem at the end of this book explained the
sad plight of Louis XVI for the cadets:

> Si l'effet chez Louis eût suivi la menace,
> Il eût facilement dompté les factieux;
> Mais toujours sa faiblesse enhardit leur audace,
> Et du meilleur des rois fit le plus malheureux.[66]

Subsequently, in 1812, Pierre Blanchard put four whole pages in
the fourth edition of his *Beautés de l'Histoire de France* listing
evidence of Louis XVI's good-heartedness. There was the story
about how he once had kept a hunting party from pursuing a stag
across a wheat field because he did not want his pleasures to harm
another person's property. After the terrible accident that injured
so many people at his marriage celebration, he sent a sympathetic
note telling the police to hurry to the aid of the most unfortunate
first. In addition, he gave money to the poor, dispensed with the
joyeux avènement, abolished the *corvée*, established the Mont-
de-Piété in Paris, and ended the preliminary torture of criminals.
Blanchard's 1812 assessment of Louis XVI became definitive; it
remained unchanged even in the book's twenty–first edition,
published in 1862, and the new revised edition of 1869.[67]

In writing about the French Revolution authors had to be
careful not to say anything that would cause dissension or malign
participants who were still living; such were the rules laid down
by Fouché.[68] Many of the events that occurred during the Revolution were described dispassionately, but others were treated in
ways that reveal a definite bias. For example, the days of October
5 and 6, 1789, were described without emphasizing the role of
women or ever mentioning bread,[69] but when they were mentioned, the women who marched to Versailles were "furious
females" or "monsters."[70] A typical passage described the procession that escorted the king back to Paris as a frightening spectacle:

"The king's carriage was preceded and followed by monsters of both sexes, dripping with blood and intoxicated; the heads of the unfortunate, massacred bodyguards were carried on the ends of pikes. Young readers, you would shudder if we faithfully retraced this scene of horrors. Ah! May you never see such a sight!"[71] Similar passages sarcastically described many other "monsters" who committed all kinds of crimes against innocent people in the name of liberty and who ironically all eventually received their just reward on the impartial scaffold.[72]

The contents of Imperial history textbooks usually included the history of the current regime. Napoleon's early career was described in detail. After the battle of Aboukir the young hero who would one day control the destiny of Europe returned to a France "which called out for a savior."[73] Some members of the Council of Ancients and Five Hundred met at the Hôtel de Salm to convert the two councils into a national convention, which would then confide the executive authority to a committee of public safety. Instead of joining this conspiracy, General Bonaparte warned the Ancients about it and had the Five Hundred convoked at St. Cloud on November 10.[74] Hence, on 18 Brumaire "Bonaparte's life was exposed to the greatest danger, but the good cause triumphed."[75] When Antoine Sérieys discussed the role Pius VII played in Napoleon's coronation, he created the impression that the two got along fabulously:

> "They believed at first that the pope would only assist at the coronation ceremony of the Emperor; he wanted to perform it himself. Friend of an extraordinary man, he took him in his arms, shed tears of joy; the souls in heaven alone could imagine what happened then in the two hearts so well made for mutual understanding. The pope consecrated, crowned his friend, his dear Napoleon, amidst religious chants and public gladness. He saw himself surrounded by a loving nation, he blessed them. And may we for a long time enjoy, in France, the graces which heaven stores up in the pontiff's heart in order to distribute them to the first children of the church!"[76]

Great emphasis was placed on Napoleon's military exploits, too. One whole textbook was devoted to Napoleon's German and Italian campaigns[77] and many others devoted several pages to this subject. Of course, the Napoleonic Code did away with the errors and abuses of previous legal practice.[78] Anglophobia also was incorporated into most textbooks, as when Girard de Propriac concluded his 1808 catechism with a question about what ought to be the wish of all good Frenchmen and wise Europeans. "To see Napoleon garner glory, to deliver the seas from English tyranny, and to have his glorious name carried by the free and independent fleets of Europe to the ends of the earth"[79] was the prescribed response. As for the Empire as an institution, early textbooks give the impression that it was something new or, at least, special. According to an 1810 textbook, however, the Empire was created when the French realized the necessity of reestablishing the monarchy and the Dynasty of Napoleon I was called the "Fourth Race of French monarchs,"[80] thus emphasizing the Empire as a continuation of the monarchy.

Finally, many textbooks contained a section on Chinese and Japanese history, as did the officially adopted wall chart of Le Prévost d'Iray, which pointed out that the Chinese emphasized filial piety and excelled in ethics.[81] The study of the history of the spread of Christianity to the Far East made its way into textbooks, perhaps stimulated by Napoleon's own interest in this subject and in sending missionaries there.[82] The idea that China had been an Egyptian colony circa 2882 B.C., because of the similarities between the Chinese language and hieroglyphics as well as the manners and customs of these two ancient civilizations, was written into both Sérieys' and Jean Picot's textbooks. Both authors acknowledged that they used the research published by a member of the Institut, Joseph de Guignes, as their authority.[83] As for the Japanese people, they were described as being slaves who originally came from China; the chief aspect of their national character was said to be cruelty; they believe that trading is a vile profession; and they are as ardent as their climate and as restless as the sea surrounding their islands.[84] The treatment of Far Eastern civilization in history textbooks kept abreast of Napoleon's current political interests and incorporated the research of members of the Institut; at the same time it propagated an especially low opinion

of the Japanese, who were considered quite inferior to the race
from which they were descended.

It is impossible to know how well Imperial children learned
any of these lessons from their textbooks or even how much
history the youngsters learned on their own from supplementary
reading at the beginning of the Age of Romanticism. But the
detailed memoir left by one Imperial schoolboy attending the
college of Blois in 1810 shows that this little fellow did not find his
textbook or his lessons on early medieval French history mean-
ingless. In fact, his textbook prepared him for appreciating additional reading and aroused his curiosity. That intellectual young-
ster was Augustin Thierry who, writing in 1840, fondly remem-
bered his childhood in his famous *Récits des Temps Merovingiens*.
When Thierry described how it happened that he chose a career
as an historian he recalled that someone brought a copy of
Chateubriand's *Les Martyrs* to the school and the pupils agreed
among themselves to take turns reading it. When his turn came,
he feigned a sore foot so he could stay indoors to read it during
recess. As he devoured the pages, he felt excited by the descriptions of Rome, the Roman court, and the Roman army encoun-
tering the Franks. Prepared by the brief lessons which he had
memorized from his textbook, *Histoire de France à l'usage des
élèves de l'Ecole militaire*, he was captivated by Chateaubriand's
description of the terrible Franks dressed in animal skins. The
more he thought about them, Thierry continued, the more excited
he became until finally, he jumped from his desk and stamped
back and forth in the vaulted classroom, repeating aloud the
words from the book; "Pharamond! Pharamond! We have fought
with the sword." Thierry's youthful enthusiasm for history gives
a picture of how a child's romantic mind took over where his
textbook left off and led him to develop an intense feeling for this
subject that lasted throughout his lifetime.[85]

Undoubtedly, Napoleon put his imprint on history education
and stimulated the imaginations of the young. The new importance the dictatorship placed on history education certainly
helped to institutionalize it into the modern curriculum but at

the same time, the new history textbooks showed that history could sometimes be used to bolster a regime. Imperial children were taught more about the world around them and less about myths of long ago. By learning about the history of France youngsters became aware of the ongoing history of their nation and were better able to consciously participate in the making of its history as citizens themselves who could uphold the Napoleonic regime. The history of the preceding one hundred years was itself molded into a new legend in the French history textbooks, which were published and gradually introduced, then successively reprinted, and in turn continued up to date, for decades after Waterloo.

Napoleon: Patron of History

Napoleon, who claimed to be a good judge of human nature, insured that history books were produced that met with his approval by using an elaborate system of rewards and punishments to manipulate Imperial historians. Naturally, some of these methods were more subtle than others, but most of them revolved around the great necessity of life in any complex society—money. Others had to do with awarding social status and prestige to worthy men as well as with simply allowing historians to follow their interests and to reach an audience.

Throughout his career Napoleon claimed to be an avid supporter of the arts. As part of this policy he assured historians that state protection and remuneration for worthy endeavors would be forthcoming. Even before the establishment of the Empire, Napoleon, as first consul, decreed that all the findings of the Egyptian expedition would be published at government expense and that the writers would share all proceeds from the sale of these books; moreover, these writers would remain on the payroll until they finished their work.[1] Other authors, such as Officer LeJeune, who wrote about the battles of Lodi and Marengo, also had their books published and sold by the government, with the writers receiving the proceeds.[2] Sometimes, however, Madame Mère's frugal nature recurred in her son, as when Napoleon expected the sales of historical works to cover the cost of publication. In this case he opposed the distribution of free copies. "That is useless," he said, "They must be sold."[3] Meanwhile, he promised to compensate the author appropriately at some future time. On more than one occasion Napoleon used psychology on sluggish historians to encourage them to finish their books on schedule—he refused to pay them until they finished the final volume and showed it to him so he could judge its merits.[4]

The compensation that Napoleon gave historians after they had demonstrated suitable ability was substantially rewarding and took several forms. The Emperor had the final word about appointments to teaching and administrative posts in the Imperial University as well as elsewhere in the government. That successful historians filled many of these posts is confirmed on the title pages of Imperial books. Napoleon also dispensed generous pensions, which ranged from 2,000 to 9,000 livres, to writers who favored the regime.[5] In addition to these compensations, Napoleon occasionally commissioned historians to write specific books for him.[6] Moreover, the creation of the Legion of Honor gave historians, along with other talented men, the hope of being selected, in this life or posthumously, for an honor that bestowed a handsome medal bearing the Emperor's profile, along with tremendous prestige, a sizable pension, and widow's and survivors' benefits for the favored one's family. Napoleon did not generally condone giving one individual more than two political jobs,[7] but he did not think that 15,000 livres was too much for one person to receive.[8]

Not only did the Emperor have a definite idea of how history should be written and how much this was worth in currency, but he also insured that his ideas were followed by establishing strict surveillance and censorship of history books.[9] Moreover, the Emperor checked the work of his surveillance personnel by doing some reading of his own, and he found that sometimes his agents disappointed his expectations while at other times they were overzealous and had to be chastened. The Emperor construed censorship as a salutary institution benefiting the commonweal.[10] All books were automatically proscribed if they were obscene or contributed to factionalism and antigovernment sentiment.[11] Censorship also was designed to insure the success of certain works and to eliminate what he called "useless" competition; such was Napoleon's conception when he decided to involve the government directly in the continuation of Velly's *Histoire de France* and *l'Abrégé chronologique* of Président Hénault: "When this work, well done and written in a good direction, has appeared, no one will have the desire or the patience to do another, especially when, far from being encouraged by the police they will be discouraged by them."[12]

"Moderation" was a key word in Napoleon's censorship policy. All kinds of historical works were censored for expressing extreme interpretations of history, but this did not always mean that they were rejected *in toto*. For example, Antoine Ferrand's book on the study of French history was allowed to go through four editions after he deleted several passages.[13] Sometimes, supplying a euphemistic title or rewriting certain passages was all that was needed to gain approval for selling a book.[14] On one occasion the Emperor did not interrupt the free sale of a history of the Directory but suggested a few details that needed correcting in future editions "for the truthfulness of history."[15] As for the author's style, what mattered to Napoleon was not that a work was poorly written but that it was credible, because "things said simply will persuade."[16] On the whole, Napoleon adhered rather consistently to the moderate policy he articulated; however, there was one area about which he seemed quite sensitive—his army. One sure way for a writer to lose his job was to describe its exploits so that the commander-in-chief thought the writer described his soldiers as monsters.[17] Moreover, to do such a thing was in the words of Napoleon "entirely indecent" and "so ignorant."[18]

Another aspect of Napoleon's patronage of historians that related closely to censorship was the publicity he gave to certain works in Imperial newspapers. If Napoleon felt that certain books were not offensive enough to suppress, but nevertheless contained some ideas that were incompatible with his overall policy, he allowed the books to appear but denied them advertising space in *Le Moniteur*.[19] In most cases this made their publication financially risky. On the other hand, if the Emperor felt that certain works could turn public opinion in a favorable direction, they were advertised for sale or subscription. Furthermore, works of exceptional excellence were given lengthy reviews in the journals and newspapers. Sometimes these reviews were so long that they were serialized and occasionally parts of full-length histories

were excerpted.[20] Napoleon's policy regarding advertising was
designed to make loyal historians more successful than others.

A special group of men to whom the Emperor gave particular
attention were the members of the Institut de France. When
Napoleon issued proclamations during the Egyptian campaign
he proudly put at the head of them: "Bonaparte, general in chief,
and member of the National Institute;" after his return he often
appeared in public wearing the prestigious, embroidered costume
bearing the silken olive branch. Once he became first consul,
then Emperor, he maintained his interest in the republic of
letters and became its official patron and protector.[21]

The Institut dated back to the Constitution of the Year III
when, after abolishing the academies of the Old Regime, the
Convention created it to perfect the arts and sciences. It consisted
of three classes under which were subsumed such varied subjects
as social science, legislation, geography, history, antiquities,
and monuments. From the beginning, however, it was proclaimed
by the Convention that the doors of this majestic, egalitarian
institution "would always be shut to intrigue. . . ." The total
membership of the Institut was fixed at 168 but this number
actually consisted of three categories of members—resident
members in Paris, corresponding members, and associated
foreigners. The original membership was provided when the
Convention named forty–eight men, who were charged with
electing the rest. A law of 29 Messidor, year IV (July 17, 1796) set
their salary at 1,500 francs; subsequently, additional money was
added to be shared by those who participated in all the meetings
held by their respective classes.[22]

According to the official history of the Institut published
during the Restoration,[23] the Class of History and Ancient Literature as such did not exist within the Institut when Napoleon came
to power. Its duties had been shared between the Class of Moral
and Political Sciences and the Class of Literature and Beaux-
Arts, with history and geography belonging to the former and
ancient literature, French and Oriental languages and literature,
and beaux arts comprising the latter. In 1802, however, the

government decided to end what was viewed as a confused arrangement and reorganized the Institut by dividing the three existing classes into the four new ones that lasted for the duration of the Napoleonic era. The decrees that created the Class of History and Ancient Literature were officially announced at a special séance of the Institut held on February 3, 1803 (15 pluviouse, an XI), in which Minister of the Interior Chaptal ordered the organization of the history class in conformity with the first consul's decrees.[24]

In spite of the reorganization, most of the rules governing the internal operations of the history class continued in effect throughout the Napoleonic era just as they had when first inaugurated by the Convention. There continued to be three categories of membership; in 1807, for example, the class consisted of forty resident members, eight associated foreigners from Europe, America, and India, and forty–six corresponding members.[25] Traditionally, the bureau of the class was run by an elected president, secretary, and one member who represented the class on the administrative commission of the entire Institut. It was the responsibility of the president to maintain order at meetings and to insure that the scholars behaved like gentlemen by refraining from making personal attacks and from indulging in abusive language or name-calling while criticizing the work of their colleagues.[26] The secretary's job was to keep a register of the minutes of meetings, to preserve copies of all reports, extracts, and the like, so that he could write a brief history of the proceedings for publication at the beginning of each of the volumes of the *Mémoires* of the class, and to write a scholarly biography of any member who died.[27] Article XI of the rules, which stated that the class should avoid all historical, religious and political discussions that by their subject or proximity could disrupt the harmonious relations existing among the members, also continued in effect.[28] The annual selection of papers for publication was still decided by committees from among the papers delivered at sessions held at various times throughout the year.[29] Finally, the only stated restrictions for nomination to the class for regular membership continued to be

that persons be French and at least twenty–five years old and
have earned a reputation for doing the kind of work for which the
class was created.[30]

Pursuant to the reorganizational decrees, the historians of the
newly created third class submitted for the first consul's approval
the names of Le Brun to serve as class president for the remainder
of the year and Dacier as *secrétaire perpétuel*. Subsequently, the
membership, which previously had submitted its internal regulations (mentioned above) for governmental sanction, devoted
several sessions to drawing up four new additional regulations
relating to their monetary compensation, as with the preceding
rules, these in turn were adopted by the class before being
submitted for final governmental approval; this was forthcoming
on 26 Floréal, year XI. What these additional regulations established was a special fund to be created by setting aside 300 francs
from each member's salary of 1,500 francs to be used to reward
those members who actively participated in meetings of the
Institut while absentees would forfeit their rights to the money.
Only those members who were public functionaries would be
exempted from the forfeiture but these men would not receive
the usual member's annual pay since their salaries would be drawn
from a special fund reserved for this use. The funds accrued from
absenteeism and the functionaries' suspended salaries were designated for special distribution among all the regular members in
the class who were both sixty years of age and currently not functionaries. Thus, the reorganization was a compromise designed
by its own membership as well as by the government. It rewarded
the elderly historians who regularly participated in the class
sessions to report on the progress of their research more than
those who were younger and/or guilty of dereliction of duty.[31]

Precisely how Napoleon construed the real duty of the historians of the Institut became clearer with the passage of time.
Almost immediately, he received a report from the police that
Delisle de Sales had written a brochure that depicted the French
Revolution badly. His decision of June 24, 1802, made his feelings
explicit: "I ask Consul Cambacérès to become knowledgeable
about this brochure, and to know why they have not prevented

this madman from writing and if there is not a way to stop this publication; and to know if they could not exclude a man who writes against the state from the Institut."[32] Thereafter, the membership was repeatedly directed to occupy itself with intellectual subjects and projects that would not allow for the Institut's being used as an antigovernmental political forum and, at last, they seem to have accepted Napoleon's message. The official records of the class made the following euphemistic disclaimer of subversive activities: "The Class, thus organized, thought only of occupying itself with works for which it had been created; and it has continued ever since without any interrruption."[33] Addressing the general assembly of the Institut in July, 1807, to give the annual report of the Third Class's research progress, Monsieur Ginguené remarked that it faithfully followed the regulations that made the Institut one big family.[34]

The class regarded itself as the successor of the Academy of Inscriptions and Belles-Lettres and claimed to follow its predecessor's scholarly principles.[35] Immediately after its creation the class was consulted by the government about inscriptions for a new minting of coins.[36] In 1806, Napoleon confided the academy's former charge of composing the inscriptions for public monuments and of proposing subjects and legends for commemorative medals to this group—something that had not been specifically assigned to it by the decrees of 1803.[37] Some of these that the class composed or was consulted about over the years were inscribed on the fountain with the lion of Saint Mark on the esplanade of the Invalides, the temporary triumphal arch erected at Etoile for the Emperor's second marriage, and the *arc de triomphe au Carrousel*. They also wrote inscriptions for a monument erected by the canal linking the Meuse and the Rhine, the obelisk erected on the eastern side of the mountain at Landsberg near Aix-la-Chapelle, and the obelisk erected by the city of Marseilles to celebrate the birth of the king of Rome.[38] The largest long–range project of this kind was attempted by a five-member committee, which between 1806 and 1815 developed a medallic history of the Empire composed of more than 250 medals with two accompanying folio-volumes of text.[39]

During late spring of the following year, 1807, the class was charged by the minister of interior with continuing the famous historical work of the Benedictines of Saint-Maur. Consequently, the class made plans to take on this project and formed a committee composed of Messieurs Ginguené, Brial, Pastoret, Dacier, de Sainte-Croix and, after the latter's death, Daunou to do the work. Since the twelve volumes the Benedictines had published left off with the twelfth century, the committee commenced their labors with that period. By 1815 they had three volumes ready for publication.[40]

Another long-range project came to final fruitation in February 1808. The first consul's decree of April 5, 1804 (13 Ventôse, year X), had charged the Institut to write a general summary of the state and progress of the sciences, letters and arts covering the period from 1789 to September 22, 1801 (1 Vendémiaire, year X). For various reasons, however, this charge had not been carried out immediately. In May, 1807, the minister of interior ordered all four classes of the Institut to complete the project without further delay, with the extra proviso that they now do this for the years 1789 through 1806. In order to expedite its share of the work, the history class assigned the project to nine of its members, who were expected to supply the information fairly and impartially for the permanent secretary, who would prepare the general draft from the committee's reports. The finished product was approved by the entire class at the end of 1807, and the document was formally accepted by the Emperor in the Council of State on February 20, 1808. His Majesty thereupon ordered three thousand copies printed.[41]

The Decennial Prizes, which were instituted on 24 Fructidor in the year XII (September 11, 1804),[42] were an important facet of Napoleon's overall plans to patronize the arts and sciences. These thirty–five prizes, nineteen of which were for 10,000 francs and sixteen for 4,000 francs, were designed to be awarded to the best works in each category. According to a subsequent Imperial decree, made on November 28, 1809,[43] works that were produced in the decade 1800–1810, would be eligible for the first distribution of prizes on November 9, 1810, the anniversary of the 18

Brumaire. The Emperor planned to award the medals personally
in a ceremony at the Tuileries. For a while Napoleon even toyed
with the idea of constructing on Montmartre a kind of temple of
Janus, to be one of the most beautiful monuments in the world, to
honor the Decennial Prize winners. He considered financing its
construction by inviting members of the electoral colleges to give
sizable donations,[44] but he never pursued this idea.

Initially, Napoleon's 1804 decree designated a jury composed
of the permanent secretaries and presidents of each of the four
classes of the Institut to select the Decennial Prize winners. The
jury was instructed to assess all of the books considered in the
competition in order to provide examples for writers to follow
and to point out faults to avoid in future works. After the jury
reported to the minister of interior, the Emperor planned formally
to announce the final decision by decree.[45] The additional decree
on the Decennial Prizes of 1809, however, involved each entire
class in the reviewing and criticism of the works.[46] Napoleon still
was not entirely satisfied with all the judging[47] and the Decennial
Prizes were not awarded as originally planned.[48] Nevertheless,
the Emperor did approve the nominations for the first–prize
winner in category eight—the best history or piece of general
history, either ancient or modern—and the extracts of the Institut's report were printed in *Le Moniteur*.[49]

At the beginning of its report the jury stated the qualities that
distinguish superior historical writing. Fidelity in the exposition
of facts was the foremost consideration but several others were
considered important and more difficult to accomplish: developing and analyzing causal relationships, achieving dramatic effects
by interweaving circumstances, giving historical figures distinctive characters and speech, and writing with style appropriate for
the subject or situation being treated. These qualities made history more interesting and useful.[50]

Among the seven books the jury deemed worthy of mention,
L'Histoire de l'anarchie de Pologne by Claude Carloman de Rulhière was designated to receive the Decennial Prize. This was an
interesting choice for several reasons. In the first place, Rulhière
had written about contemporary events. Moreover, he had been

commissioned by the French government to write his history with a French bias, and he was faithful to his instructions. The jury summarized the thesis of the book as the action of courageous nobles struggling for national independence from foreign domination and concomitantly, for conservation of their privileges. They commented that ordinarily a book written in such a frame of mind would be suspect; however, this was not a serious reproach in this particular instance because "in serving the political system of France, Rulhière upheld the best cause." Finally, the jury concluded its critique by saying that in spite of the fact that Rulhière was not objective—"the most serious defect for which a historian can be upbraided"—and that he made some factual errors, his book on the history of anarchy in Poland was incontrovertibly one of the best books in the French language.[51] The jury never mentioned the fact that Napoleon was responsible for its publication posthumously, in 1807.[52]

The projects on the literary history of France, Imperial medals, and the Decennial Prizes were only some of the cooperative ventures the Third Class tackled during the Empire. Similar group efforts resulted in the publication of the seventh and eighth volumes of the *Notices and Extraits des Manuscrits de la Bibliothèque du Roi et autres Bibliothèques*, the compilation of two additional volumes of the *Historiens de France*, and the fifteenth volume of the *Ordonnances des Rois de France de la troisième race*.[53]

On an individual basis members of the history class busied themselves with various research topics, most of which were in medieval European or Asian history. For example, during the year 1809, while committees worked on the collected ordinances of French kings and Imperial medals, other historians were working independently on such topics as: a French translation of Heeren's *The Influence of the Crusades*;[54] the Peace of Vervins of 1598; public revenues in France from the beginning of the third dynasty to Louis XI's reign; a twelfth–century manuscript written by Hugues de Cleers; and a letter to Adele, daughter of William the Conqueror.[55] Others were doing research on the influence of Islam in the Middle East, the Assassins,[56] and the histories of

China and India.[57] While these members of the Institut were upholding French scholarly traditions established long before the Revolution,[58] they were also researching topics that conformed with His Majesty's interests as expressed in his correspondence. Incidentally, Messieurs Langlès, Silvestre de Sacy, and Amédée Jaubert were also teaching Persian, Arabic, and Turkish, respectively, at the Ecole Spéciale des Langues Orientales Vivantes at the Bibliothèque Impériale,[59] while M. de Guignes was commissioned by the Emperor to write a Chinese dictionary.[60]

An additional incentive for members of the Institut was the distribution of other prizes. Each year the members of the Class of History and Ancient Literature could compete for a prize of 1,500 francs for the best essay on an announced subject. In addition to the money, the winner was sent on an all–expense–paid trip to the Academy of France at the Medici Villa in the balmy and scenic eternal city of Rome.[61]

The class' predecessor—the Class of Moral and Political Sciences—had selected four topics for prize competition:

1. What was the influence of the Lutheran Reformation on the political situation of the various states of Europe, and on the progress of enlightenment?

2. To what extent does the barbarous treatment of animals affect public morality and is it advisable to make laws prohibiting such treatment?

3. How has the progressive abolition of servitude in Europe influenced the development of the enlightenment and wealth of nations?

4. How should the faculty of thinking be broken down, and what are the elemental faculties that ought to be recognized therein?

The results were to be announced during the years XII and XIII. Before the prizes could be awarded, however, Napoleon ordered the restructuring of the classes of the Institut. The new history and ancient literature class thereafter decided that it should follow through with the awarding of the much–publicized prizes. The prize for the best essay on the influence of the Lutheran Reformation went to Charles Villers, a professor at the University of Göttingen who a short time later became a corresponding member of the Institut. None of the many essays submitted on the second and third questions were judged meritorious enough to receive the prize and these questions were simply abandoned. The fourth question pertaining to the process of thinking was extended for another year; that time the prize was given to M. Maine-Biran, who subsequently also became a corresponding member of the Institut.[62]

The first prize competition actually established by the history class itself was more in keeping with the members' interests and the direction in which the Emperor encouraged the class to go— "a critical examination of the sources and the use of these sources which George le Syncelle employed to write his *chronographie*." The prize went to M. le Prévost d'Iray, censor of studies at the Lycee Impériale.[63]

Because the class found none of the 1806 essay entries satisfactory, that subject was extended for an additional year. Finally, the winner of that competition on the subject of "an examination of the administration of Egypt from the conquest of it by Augustus until the taking of Alexandria by the Arabs, taking into account during this interval the condition of the Egyptians and exposing the condition of foreigners, particularly that of the Jews" was once again M. le Prévost d'Iray.[64]

Of the two questions posed for 1808, "What was the influence of the Crusades on the civil liberty of the peoples of Europe, on their civilization, and on the progress of enlightenment, commerce and industry?" ended in a tie between Maxime de Choiseul-d'Aillecourt and Monsieur Heeren of the University of Göttingen. The other prize for "an examination of what during the first three centuries of the hegira had been the influence of Mohammedanism on the spirit, manners and government of the peoples who adopted this religion" was not awarded but in 1809 it was given to Monsieur Olsner, who represented the Senate of the Republic of Bremen in France.[65]

The year 1810 was an optimum one for the amount of prize money distributed. One subject for a regular prize that year was an involved question: "Under the government of the Goths, what was the civil and political state of the peoples of Italy? What were the fundamental principles of the legislation of Theodoric and his successors; and more especially, what were the distinctions made

between the vanquishers and the vanquished?" The prize for this
went to another Göttingen professor, George Sartorius. In this
specific instance, however, something unusual happened; because
another essay was deemed worthy of some reward, the minister
of interior produced a sum of 1,000 francs as a special second
prize for Joseph Naudet, a professor at the Lycée Napoléon. In
addition, that same year the class offered another prize on a
second topic, "the examination of the historians of Alexis Com-
nena and of the three princes of his family who succeeded him, in
which one ought to compare these writers with the historians of
the Crusades, without neglecting what Arab authors said about
these reigns and these emperors, and principally on their policy
towards the Crusaders." This prize was shared between two
equally worthy but dissimilar *mémoires*. One author was Frederick
Wilken, a history professor at the University of Heidelberg, and
the other was Monsieur le Prévost d'Iray, who had already won
the competitions for 1805 and 1806 while he was associated with
the administration of the Lycée Impérial, but who meanwhile
had advanced to the position of inspector general of the Imperial
University. In all, the money distributed as a result of these
contests during 1810 amounted to 4,000 francs, a notable increase
over the 1,500 francs that usually was the annual inducement.[66]
Perhaps the sudden increase was related to the cancellation of
the Decennial Prizes formerly scheduled for this year.

The last subject of an annual concourse during the First
Empire was for the year 1811: "What peoples inhabited Cisalpine
and Transalpine Gaul in the various historical epochs before
A.D. 410; where had their capital cities been located and what
was the extent of the territories which they occupied; trace the
successive changes which took place in the division of the provinces of the Gauls." The prize was awarded to Monsieur Walck-
enaer, who afterward was named to membership in the history
class.[67]

This summation of the essay competitions held between 1805
and 1811 indicates that historians who already belonged to the
class never won any of them; rather, prizes were won either by
historians on the staffs of French *lycées* and the Imperial Uni-

versity or by professors at the German universities of Göttingen
or Heidelberg, who after winning the concourse normally were
named to the Institut either as regular or corresponding members.
Thus, the contests had significance as part of Napoleon's patronage system inasmuch as they usually singled out individuals for
the receipt of these as well as of additional honors. It also indicates
the degree of interaction that existed between the historians of
the Institut and Napoleon. After the class selected the most
talented authors for prizes, Napoleon was able to appoint these
persons to fill out the membership on the basis of their proven
merit. Moreover, he knew in advance that their peers would
approve of them because they had already indicated as much by
awarding them the prizes.

The protection of copyrights was a final aspect of Napoleon's
patronage system. Initially, Napoleon extended the old copyright law that had been passed by the National Convention on
July 19, 1793, giving proprietary rights to authors while they
lived and to their heirs for ten years. The Imperial decree of
February 5, 1810, reconfirmed this with a new stipulation extend-
ing heirs' ownership rights for twenty years.[68] A few years later a
project was prepared to protect the copyrights of Imperial continuators of published works. Authors whose continuations com-
prised at least one–fourth of a book could copyright the entire
work without infringing upon the original author's patent.[69]
Hence, Imperial historians as well as authors and continuators of
any kind of book could expect to receive increased royalties from
their publications.

In conclusion, the historical profession during the Empire
had both rewarding and unattractive features. Historical censorship was moderate inasmuch as writers who failed to meet
Imperial standards were not threatened with physical punish-
ment or imprisoned. In fact, they had little to lose except the
revenues they might have made if their histories had been
published and sold successfully. But censorship was thorough
and ever present. On the other hand, Napoleon's patronage
system meant that historians stood to profit greatly if they could
demonstrate to the emperor that they possessed both the inclina-

tion and ability. Persons of talent could do well financially, and Napoleon catered to their needs for prestige and social distinctions as well. Moreover, some aspects of Napoleon's patronage were designed to improve the quality of subsequent historical works. Certainly the members of the Institut and other historians commissioned by the government were able to devote more of their time to careful research in ancient and medieval history than would have been possible if the demands of making a living had forced them to pursue their investigations as an avocation. Napoleon's methods seem to have worked effectively because, whenever the Emperor ordered Fouché to engage a historian to do a specific job, someone with the necessary talent was always discovered. Although the members of the Institut did not admit it, their work also indicates that Napoleon manipulated them successfully. Through his institution Napoleon became the patron of historians of merit whether they resided in France, Germany, or around the world.

Imperial Historians

While Napoleon made history, others wrote it by his encouragement and dictation. Although his brilliant career outshone their sedentary efforts, an examination of their individual lives and writings sheds light on the historical profession and the intellectual life of the Empire. It also reveals how the Emperor's idea of history was actually applied in practice.

There are many problems to overcome in selecting representative Imperial historians. In the first place, history as a discipline was not clearly defined at the beginning of the Empire. Nor were there established criteria for selecting the best historians, because Napoleon's historical policies evolved gradually. Another problem relates to secondary works. Historians have been superficial in their treatment of Imperial historians, whom they insist are not worth examining thoroughly. This attitude has carried over to bibliographers, who frustrate the serious Napoleonic scholar by omitting details they assume nobody is interested in knowing. There are also problems concerning the authorship of history books published during the Empire. Many authors, such as Velly, Mably, Count Ségur, and Rulhière, were enjoying posthumous careers. Famous authors are, of course, immediately recognizable, but unwary investigators are prey for more obscure writers because often posthumously published histories were also posthumously written; that is, they were continued by Imperial historians who gave full credit to the original author. For example, *Instruction sur l'Histoire de France et sur l'histoire romaine . . . jusqu'à l'heureux retour de Louis XVIII* was attributed to Abbé Le Ragois, who died in 1683.[1] Furthermore, acts of piracy and charlantanry were committed. Nevertheless, there were some historians who, for various reasons, seem representative of the caliber of historians in Napoleonic France.

Some of the most important work in the field of French antiquities was done by Marie-Alexandre Lenoir (1761–1839), who was the creator and conservator of the Musée des Monuments Français. Far from being dry as dust, Lenoir's early career as an antiquary was virtually a struggle against radical revolutionary forces as he applied himself to saving the remnants of the Gothic past. In 1790 Lenoir was able to persuade the National Assembly to retain all the art objects confiscated from the churches and convents in the national domain, and the cloister of the Petits-Augustins was designated as their depository. In 1793 Lenoir came into conflict with the iconoclasts who wanted to destroy his treasures and melt the bronzes for armaments and coins. By acting decisively Lenoir was able to save about a hundred of his monuments with the cooperation of the Commune and the Committee of Public Safety. On 12 Vendémiaire in the year III (October 3, 1794), the Musée des Monuments Français was opened to the public and Lenoir catalogued it. But the *musée* was not an immediate success because current public taste preferred classical antiques.[2]

The establishment of the Consulate and the Empire coincided with a shift in public taste away from classical antiquity[3] toward things French.[4] This brought an improvement in the conditions under which Lenoir worked. Lucien Bonaparte, as minister of the interior, appointed Lenoir to serve as administrator of the enlarged Musée des Monuments Français that was created in the Louvre. Lenoir was also put in charge of the treasures at Malmaison, where he decorated the park. For the duration of the Empire Lenoir continued to enrich the museum collection.[5]

In order to interest the public in visiting his collection, Lenoir compiled catalogues of the various relics, giving a description of each item and its history. The catalogues, which sold for as little as three francs at the *musée*,[6] were bound separately and also as part of the *Mémoires de l'Académie celtique*.[7] In addition, excerpts from the catalogue were occasionally published in *Le Moniteur*.[8] Even English–speaking people could read about France's great monuments by purchasing an English edition, which had two hundred and fifty engravings and sold for seventy–eight francs.[9]

The Musée des Monuments Français was a great success during the Empire, and the importance and the usefulness of these collections could be judged by the crowds from France and abroad who visited and revisited it.[10] For these people Lenoir made the French past come alive, as the historian Jules Michelet later attested. Michelet, who was born in 1798, said he became enamored of history when, as a small child, he visited the *musée*. As an adult he still recalled how going from room to room, as if from age to age, peering at the pale faces of the marble sleepers stretched out on their tombs, made his heart palpitate.[11] Unfortunately, the Bourbon Restoration could not tolerate the institution Lenoir had created. Because it flourished under the Empire, Louis XVIII suppressed it.[12]

The fact that some Imperial historians published many works is certainly proven by the career of another writer, Antoine Sérieys (1755–1819). This most prolific of all Imperial historians produced sixty–four works during the course of his sixty–four year life and these filled about one hundred and fifty volumes.[13] But other details about his career are interesting, too.

As a young man Sérieys went to Paris in 1779 to make his fortune.[14] Marmontel and d'Alembert helped him find his first employment, but he seems to have disappointed the expectations of his early patrons. After visiting Italy in 1780, he opened a school in Paris, but this venture failed. After Bailly became mayor of Paris he gave Sérieys a position in one of the book depots, which at first supplied monasteries and later stored confiscated books and manuscripts. His first publications, which were poetry, appeared in 1789.[15] In 1794, Sérieys advanced to become the head of the book depository, where he continued to work. In 1795, Sérieys' career took a turn toward the historical profession. In that year he published a four–volume history of the French Republic[16] and became professor of history at the Institut des Boursiers, which later became the Prytanée Français. In a dedicatory letter he wrote in 1806 to Fourcroy, who was then director general of public instruction, Sérieys said that he had taught Fourcroy's son at that institution.[17] However, Sérieys soon lost this position because of misconduct. During 1798 and 1799 he taught the second–year course, "Morale, Explication des Droits et des Devoirs de l'Homme et du Citoyen," at the Lycée Louis-le-Grand.[18]

The creation of the Empire does not seem to have affected Sérieys' career adversely. While he worked in the bureau of public instruction in the Ministry of the Interior, he wrote a history textbook, *Tablettes chronologiques à l'usage du Prytanée Français*, for the Commission des Livres Classiques[19] and in 1803, the commission made it one of the three official history texts for use in government schools.[20] About this time, however, Sérieys seems to have been hard pressed for funds. His friend, Abbé Sicard,[21] whose life he had saved during the Revolution, allowed Sérieys to put his more famous name on several works to make them sell better.[22] Several of Sérieys' works appeared with Sicard's name on them during this period of his life. In 1804, Sérieys received a new appointment as censor of studies and professor of history at Douai. He kept this post only a year and then was appointed as censor at the *lycée* of Cahors, but this job too was of short duration. In 1805, another of Sérieys' history textbooks was adopted by the government. This one was a précis and continuation of Président Hénault's *Histoire de France*, which Sérieys continued to Napoleon's coronation.[23] Sérieys' financial problems may not have been solved, for he resorted to fabricating books and then attributing their authorship to other very famous people. He also published some of the manuscripts he found in the book depository where he had worked. Furthermore, in order to produce a successful history he pirated one of Raynal's works, for which he created an original preliminary discourse. In 1806, when he wrote the third edition of the textbook the commission had adopted in 1803, he claimed that he had corrected the errors that had been pointed out to him by certain professors and "especially by one of my former pupils, who to take some rest from the wear and tear of the palace, indulges in the study of history."[24] In 1809, Sérieys received some favorable publicity when his name appeared in the *Moniteur* among the list of persons appointed by the Emperor to fill vacancies on the staff of the recently organized Imperial University.[25] On this occasion Napo-

leon made him professor of history and secretary of the faculty at
the Academy of Douai, where he had taught briefly several years
earlier; he still held this post in 1811. In 1814, Sérieys was back in
Paris, where he continued to turn out books until he died, presumably pen in hand, in 1819. Sérieys' publishing success was not
spoiled by the Restoration; he continued to publish just as he had
during the Revolution and the Empire.[26] Moreover, his death
did not quell the flow of his writings, which continued to appear;
his history textbooks were still being "officially adopted" and
published as such in 1822.[27]

Although some details of Sérieys' life remain obscure, his biography has some interesting implications. First of all, he apparently lacked what twentieth–century historians would call professional integrity or honesty, for he literally begged, borrowed,
and stole historical compositions, in addition to developing his
own original creations. Nevertheless, his works circulated freely
during his lifetime, and more editions of them appeared posthumously. During the Empire Sérieys held several teaching positions, though all very briefly. Despite his instability, Napoleon
gave this itinerant a post in the Imperial University. The only
explanation seems to be that Sérieys used his personal connec-
tions with friends and former students, one of whom, perhaps,
may have been Napoleon himself. Yet, with all these publications
and jobs Sérieys was never well off financially. Moreover, Napoleon never gave him special honors. Sérieys wrote history in a
glorious age when some men's service to the state received great
fanfare and brought them great honors, but the prolific bookmaker
was a poor, unimportant person who, with all his faults, worked
hard all of his life without really progressing socially or financially.
Ironically, Sérieys' influence on the historical consciousness of a
generation of French youth, who studied history from the textbooks he put together, is incalculable. Sérieys' publications record
also suggests how subtly Napoleon's influence on French education extended into the Restoration, in spite of the conservatives'
efforts to eradicate the past.

The majority of Napoleon's historians, however, were not
antiquarians or hacks like Sérieys, but more conventional his-

torians like Jean-Charles-Dominque de Lacretelle, called Lacretelle the Younger (1766–1855). Lacretelle became very popular, and his was one of the most distinguished careers of any Imperial historian.

Lacretelle became a lawyer when he was eighteen years old. In 1787 he went to Paris to work with his older brother Pierre on the *Encyclopédie méthodique*.[28] Lacretelle remained in Paris after the Revolution began and covered the sessions of the Constituent Assembly for the *Journal des Débats*.[29] In 1790 he became secretary to La Rochefoucould-Liancourt and as part of his employment helped the philosopher write his *Mémoires*. Lacretelle then joined the staff of Suard's *Journal de Paris*, on which André Chénier worked. After the fall of Robespierre, Lacretelle became a leader of the *jeunesse dorée*, and he participated in the royalist movement of the 13 Vendémiaire.[30] On 18 Fructidor in the year V (September 4, 1797), Lacretelle was arrested on the charge of being a royalist and he spent twenty–three months in prison.[31] Like Sir Walter Raleigh, Lacretelle passed his time by writing history. The result was his *Précis de l'histoire de La Révolution*, which was a continuation of a work began by Rabaut Saint-Etienne.

Lacretelle's later attachment to the Empire may be said to date from his prison sentence, because Fouché was responsible for freeing him.[32] Lacretelle came over willingly to the Bonapartist cause.[33] However, Napoleon must not have trusted him completely because after the 18 Brumaire Lacretelle was barred from the Tribunate by the first consul. In 1800, Lacretelle was made a member of the bureau of the press.[34] While he was working there Lacretelle turned historian, under the influence of Pierre-Louis Roederer,[35] and began to publish his five–volume *Précis historique de la Révolution française*, which he completed in 1806. In 1807, this work caught the attention of the Emperor, who sent Fouché a penetrating letter on this subject: "It seems to be written in a good spirit," he wrote, before pointing out one minor error of fact that needed correcting—"That is the only thing which struck me."[36] Shortly after this nod of approval from Napoleon, Lacretelle also published a history textbook—*Leçons élé-*

mentaires de l'histoire de France, depuis Pharamond jusqu'à l'anné 1807, *à l'usage des enfants des deux sexes*—which sold for one franc.[37]

Lacretelle published the first two volumes of his *magnum opus, Histoire de France pendant le XVIIIe siècle*, in 1808. This work received much publicity from the government. M. Roger gave a verbose, laudatory discourse before the *corps législatif* on December 14, 1808, in which he recommended that Lacretelle's book be put in their library.[38] The book also attracted the attention of the Emperor, who succinctly expressed his opinion of it to Fouché: "It seems, in general, well written and done in a good spirit." But the Emperor could not resist the temptation to add: "There would be no harm to hold the pitiful and snivelling style of the ministers of Holland up to ridicule. That needs to be done with a little tact."[39] Michaud gave these two volumes a favorable review in the *Journal Général*, although he criticized Lacretelle's style, which he thought sometimes lacked color and vigor.[40]

Lacretelle's career as a historian now showed signs of great promise. In 1809 Napoleon named him adjunct-professor of history in the Faculty of Letters at the University of Paris. Lacretelle's history failed to win the nomination for the Decennial Prize in 1810, but it gained honorable mention.[41] Perhaps, to compensate for this disappointment, and for losing his place as editor of the *Publiciste* when it was amalgamated with the *Gazette de France*,[42] Lacretelle was made an Imperial censor at a salary of 1,200 francs annually.[43] In 1811, Napoleon bestowed additional favors upon Lacretelle. When Joseph Chénier, who had been commissioned by the police to continue Abbé Millot's textbook *Eléments de l'histoire de France*, died, Napoleon agreed with Fouché's proposal that Lacretelle assume this important task. But in lieu of the 6,000 francs that Chénier had been paid, Napoleon merely promised to pay Lacretelle according to the merits of the completed textbook.[44] Lacretelle subsequently accepted Napoleon's appointment to the Institut. Finally, in 1812, he was promoted to the rank of professor in the Faculty of Letters. Now, in addition to the proceeds from his popular books, Lacre-

telle held three important posts—professor, censor, and academician—for the duration of the Empire; yet, Napoleon never
deemed him a truly great historian: "Many phrases . . . and little
color; no results; he is an academician, and not a historian."[45]

Lacretelle's actions after Napoleon's first abdication suggest a
reason other than his talent that may have led the Emperor to
give him the "Imperial" treatment. Lacretelle immediately voiced
his royalist sentiments so strongly that he himself later made
recantations in his books. He remained in the limelight during
the First Restoration and it was he who presented the members
of the French Academy to Tsar Alexander I on April 11, 1814. In
October of that same year Lacretelle was appointed *censeur royal*,
a position he had occupied during the Empire. As might be
expected, during the Hundred Days he took a hurried trip to
Ghent. After being reassured by Fouché, his old benefactor,
Lacretelle returned to Paris. When Louis XVIII was finally
restored, Lacretelle continued to work for the government as a
censor, to write historical works, to teach at the university, and to
work in the academy, just as he had done during the Empire.[46]

The historical works Lacretelle the Younger wrote during the
Empire earned him a reputation for being a precursors of the great
nineteenth–century French historians.[47] His *Précis historique de
la Révolution française* was not a detailed work, nor did the author
say that he intended it to be. His main object, he said, was "to
show the French Revolution, which towers above all others, and
a man who towers above the revolution."[48] Nevertheless, this
book won a reputation for being the first continuous narrative
history of the French Revolution, which subsequently inspired
other more famous writers, including Adolphe Thiers.[49]

Lacretelle's *L'Histoire de France pendant le XVIIIe siècle* was
better than his précis of the Revolution, although even his colleagues in the Institut were aware of its shortcomings. First of all, as
they stated in their report, which appeared in *Le Moniteur*,
because it was based simply upon the work of Saint-Simon,
Voltaire, and Duclos, many facts remained obscure and inexact.
Moreover, it was often uncritical and superficial, especially when
dealing with political considerations. Finally, it ignored the

causes of most events while it included too many anecdotes, which were not in keeping with "the dignity of history."[50] Thus, the historians of the Institut judged the work of their peer in 1810, and they were quite correct in saying that some parts of Lacretelle's history of the eighteenth century lacked dignity and analysis. In fact, a careful reading of his footnotes suggests that Lacretelle sometimes spiced up his work by including anecdotes that were unnecessary to the development of the historical account. For example, when he described Frederick the Great's youth and how angry Frederick William became upon learning of his son's escape, Lacretelle inserted a footnote with an anecdote from Voltaire's *Mémoires* in which the mischievous philosophe reported that Frederick William beat his daughter so severely for helping her brother escape that he gave her a bruise under her left breast. Voltaire said he knew this for a fact because the young woman had showed him the bruise![51] While it is interesting to learn that Voltaire boasted about his enjoyable life at the Prussian court, all of this story is hardly germane to the life history of Frederick the Great. Lacretelle's retelling of it shocked his stuffier contemporaries, who were concerned about maintaining Clio's dignity.

In spite of such shortcomings, the first two volumes of Lacretelle's eighteenth–century history of France had redeeming qualities that did not pass unnoticed. As M. Roger explained to the *corps législatif*, unlike historians of the regency or the reign of Louis XV who tended to treat isolated events, Lacretelle used the advantages of hindsight which enabled him to present the events of that period in relation to the rest of subsequent French history. "Witness and victim of our disasters, he described the presumed causes of them forcefully, but without exaggeration, with gravity, but without dullness, and he strewed his recitation with ingenious traits and piquant views, without the uncalled–for aid of epigrams of wit."[52]

In conclusion, Lacretelle's work was not profound but as an observer of life and as a writer he was talented. As for his teaching career, it has been established that during the 1820s Lacretelle enjoyed a reputation as a great teacher.[53] Although he lost his position as dramatic censor in 1827, he was able to retain the chair of history to which Napoleon appointed him through successive political regimes until 1848. His years as "Napoleon's historian" were just the beginning of a long academic career during which he continued the work he started with the Emperor's patronage.

The career of another of Napoleon's historians, Pierre-Nicholas Chantreau (1741–1808), who devoted his life to promoting history as a science, ended at the height of Imperial glory. Chantreau's family had been lawyers for generations. Although he was born in France, as a young child he was taken to Spain where he lived for forty years. He taught French at the Royal Military School of Avila, and he composed a popular Spanish–French grammar textbook, which earned him an appointment to the Spanish Royal Academy.[54] Possibly because of his anticlerical and philosophical opinions Chantreau returned to France in 1782, where he continued to follow the occupation of professor.

During the Revolution Chantreau led an active political life and demonstrated strong anticlericalism. In 1792 he undertook a secret mission to the Spanish frontier where he surveyed the émigrés. When the *écoles centrales* were organized, he was named professor of history in the department of Gers.[55] During the year III his interesting pedagogical work—*Manuel des Instituteurs*—was published.[56] In addition to public–school teaching, beginning in 1796 he edited the departmental newspaper.[57] Thus as the Consulate began, Chantreau's historical career was neither separated from politics nor particularly illustrious.

Under Napoleon's government Chantreau gave up politics and devoted himself entirely to history, producing a steady flow of completed works. In 1802, he published the prospectus for a book on the importance of the study of history and the true manner of teaching it.[58] The following year, François de Neufchâteau obtained the history professorship for him at the Ecole Militaire de Fontainebleau.[59] There, he began writing his savant and instructive three–volume work, the *Science de l'Histoire*,[60] which he completed in 1806, along with another chronology of French history.[61] During his three years at Fontainebleau he also published a textbook on the elements of military history[62] before he relocated to Saint-Cyr in 1807. Finally, a month before his death he finished another two–volume textbook on the history of France from the Gauls up to September, 1808.[63]

Several of Chantreau's sixteen publications are particularly interesting because they contain many ideas on education and about the study of history, which later were commonly held or shared by other intellectuals during the Empire, including Napoleon himself. *Manuel des Instituteurs*, published in the year III, was one of the earliest of these; from this, for example, it is clear that he understood the distinction between the historian and the historiographer,[64] that he believed that morality is learned through the study of history and that prior to studying history advantageously it is necessary to learn the basic elements of history consisting of the great divisions of time and the main characters of these periods. In this teacher's manual Chantreau also mentioned that in spite of the voluminous writings of men like Rollin, de Thou, Velly, and others, contemporary knowledge of history was inexact but he could no resist his natural inclination to defend Voltaire and Gibbon as men of unparalleled talent whose philosophically written works should not be condemned for occasional factual errors since the worthy authors were seeking "man" in history. Furthermore, Chantreau believed that the writing of the entire body of history was such a difficult and enormous task that unless the government subsidized it, as well as watched over it, it would never be achieved. Such an enterprise would require specialists to write each portion with complete expertise; hence a soldier ought to write the military history or a jurist the legislative. All would have to be salaried by the Republic in order to emphasize quality rather than quantity in their production, to completely free them from the need to make a living, and to make them devout Republicans working to enlighten future generations of free men. When this happened, of course, the Republic would hire historians and not historiographers—that "parasitical and sheepish species" which monarchs support along with "the rest of the animals in their menageries."[65] Thus, Chantreau's manual, written while Napoleon was still an obscure soldier of the Revolution, gave a rationale for the establishment of a governmental patronage system in a republican society much like the one the Emperor contemplated creating during the Consulate and Empire. Moreover, Chantreau's early manual touched upon the idea that history is a science—an idea that both he and the Emperor after him subsequently developed more fully.

Chantreau's *Manuel* was quite explicit about the need to modernize the schools. Republican teachers, he said, should discard the methods they were taught previously and develop ideas better suited to the new era. They should remember how they wasted seven or eight years learning that useless jargon their teachers called the language of Cicero, memorizing lists of Roman consuls and locating cities like Athens, Syracuse, or Carthage, while they knew nothing about their own country and mother tongue. Persuaded by their own hard experiences, teachers should abjure those dangerous old principles of education and that imbecile routine in order to make education useful.[66]

To train the new Republican teaching corps, Chantreau advocated that Rivard's old project for establishing four teachers' colleges with one–year and two–year programs for elementary and secondary teachers be revived. Each of these normal schools would accommodate three hundred teachers ranging in age from twenty–five to forty, with two coming from each district. At the school the teachers would be divided into classes and take turns practice-teaching under the supervision of four commissar-instructors, who would distribute notebooks and make assignments. Those who remained a second year to become secondary teachers would study practical subjects such as astronomy, geography, morality, and history. After graduation the best graduates would be assigned to schools in the larger communes, provided they had good Republican mentalities as well as good manners and moral qualities; such precaution would be necessary "to keep from locking the wolf in the sheepfold."[67]

Finally, Chantreau's *Manuel* stated his ideas about the surveillance of the schools. He thought that the French Republic should follow the examples of the Russian and Chinese governments,

each of which already had a branch of government solely occupied
with overseeing education. Eight commissars should be hired
annually to tour the national schools, spending a month in each of
the departments. They would be responsible to the Commission
of Public Instruction and would watch teachers, examine new job
applicants, and question pupils to ascertain the loyalty of their
teachers. In addition, these commissars would check libraries
and book depots and file annual reports on the need for additional
textbooks in each depot.[68] Obviously, Chantreau did not think
that academic freedom was compatible with the establishment of
a durable Republican society nor did he see any contradiction in
adapting the despotic surveillance methods of countries to which
the Revolution had not yet spread.

Almost a decade later, in 1803, Chantreau published another
interesting item—the *Mappemonde chronographique*.[69] This was
actually a wall chart about 28 × 36 inches with parallel columns
showing at a glance the different revolutions of states and empires
mentioned in the study of ancient and modern European, African,
and Asian history from 1800 B.C. to A.D. 1800. It was a highly
simplified chart, which Chantreau colored so young eyes could
immediately perceive changes in governments or empires. To
help teachers use this chart Chantreau published a short guide
saying that such tables were being used with great success in all
branches of education and that he was confident that by using the
Mappemonde chronographique and this guide any teacher in just
a few days could teach pupils principles about the origin of
peoples, the foundation of states, and their revolutions. He
claimed that his chart was superior to existing ones, notably to
Barbeau de la Bruyère's, because its design was less complicated
(to keep the youngsters' eyes from wandering to minute details)
and was therefore more easily comprehended. At the same time,
he included additional facts in the accompanying 108–page guide
so the teacher knew how to explain fully the chart and could
supply more details if he so desired.[70]

All of Chantreau's earlier ideas about the science of history
finally crystalized into his three–quarto–volume work bearing
that title, which he dedicated to the first consul. The contents of

the first volume are remarkable for several reasons. First of all, the preliminary discourse contains a long statement of the author's belief in the practicality of historical studies because this subject shows us the political and moral bases on which states repose and helps us to judge how societal forces can be strengthened or severed. Moreover, it teaches how to distinguish truth, about our obligation to respect truth, and to know and love justice. Finally, he said, history gives us identity and roots, by joining the known to the unknown.[71] Unfortunately, he continued, there still were people who merely regarded the study of history as an agreeable pastime. This prejudice, which was born and nurtured in the colleges, still impeded the progress of historical science.[72]

Chantreau also blamed bad teaching methods for the fact that history did not yet occupy its rightful place in education; teachers wrongly considered history an exercise in memorization rather than in reasoning. But the real way to begin teaching this subject was not by giving such and such a history, but to prepare the pupil for reading. As Voltaire observed, to find in history instructive lessons and to be able to make comparisons and to draw parallels, it is not only necessary to acquire basic notions, but to adopt a mode of reading that enlightens us about the nature of the facts and inductions that can be drawn from them. Moreover, we need to be able to discard prejudices acquired from our times, our education, our political views, and the like, and read objectively.[73] Chantreau quoted Voltaire to teach an historical method that is termed historicist.

Some of the footnotes in the *Science de l'Histoire* are quite long and contain fascinating revelations of the author's mentality. One especially long footnote in the preface contains a capsule history of the study of history, as he saw it. To begin, Chantreau went back to the sixteenth century and evaluated Jean Bodin's *Méthode pour étudier l'Histoire*, which appeared in 1566. According to Chantreau, this was a treatise that could be useful to teachers who already knew how to develop the ideas it contained. After Bodin, Chantreau mentioned an anonymous work he also thought was significant—the 1655 work entitled *Science de l'Histoire*; however, Chantreau was critical of this work, of about two hundred pages, which he said "does not correspond to the title." The third work Chantreau listed was the two-volume *Méthode pour etudier l'Histoire* . . . by Nicolas Lenglet-Dufresnoi but this was also a tasteless compilation, in his opinion, which completely failed to live up to its title. Then, Chantreau singled out six eighteenth–century writers who made noteworthy contributions to the study of history: Abbé Paul Le Lorrain de Vallemont, Henry Saint-John the Viscount of Bolingbrook, the philosopher Abbé Etienne Bonnet de Condillac, the chemist Joseph Priestley, Charles Volney, and Antoine-François Ferrand. It is noteworthy that in the fine print of this footnote, which he published in 1803, Chantreau recognized Jean Bodin as a kind of "father" of historical studies. Recent research has established Bodin and other sixteenth–century French *politiques* as founders of a supposedly dead–end school of historians who were historicists three centuries before the "discovery" of scientific history by the German school at Göttingen.[75] Another important point Chantreau reveals here is that he probably got the idea for the title of his book—*Science de l'Histoire*—from one of the same name published in the seventeenth century. Then he shows that he was familiar with the notable works of subsequent seventeenth and eighteenth–century historians, including his contemporaries, whom he praises or derides according to their merits. Furthermore, by including all of this information in this manner, Chantreau forcefully makes the point that in order to avoid digressions, Imperial historians should use explanatory footnotes.

Chantreau was always careful to identify his sources. Because he used over 239 authors as well as twenty–five works known only by their titles, he listed them alphabetically. Of these, he said, he consulted Montesquieu, Filanghieri, Hume, Gibbon, Robertson, Voltaire, Condillac, Mallet, Volney, and Delisle-Desales, all of whom when they wrote on or about history painted men impartially from the perspective of their own times and let no nuance escape them.[76] In addition, he used the works most commonly found in public school libraries that he thought should be considered as classics, such as those of Rollin, Velly, Millot, Lévesque, Anquetil, and Hardion.[77] Chantreau also consulted primary sources such as *Le Moniteur universel*, the *Recueil des Ordonnances des Rois de France*, the *Procès-verbaux des Assemblées Constituantes*, and the works of Frederick the Great, Bacon, Erasmus, Pascal, Béze, and d'Aubigné. Some of the more recent writers on his list were Gaillard, Kock, and Volney, and Rabaut St. -Etienne, Ségur, and Lacretelle the Younger, who wrote on the French Revolution.[78]

In composing his text Chantreau tried to practice what he preached by writing more objectively than his predecessors, something he found especially necessary in narrating religious history. For example, Chantreau says that where Velly and Lenglet-Dufresnoi made the following entry for the year 1532: "Calvin secretly taught his errors . . ." he wrote in his own chronology: "Calvin began to make his religious opinions known. . . ." Furthermore, to keep the credulous reader from being easily taken by unverifiable facts drawn from unconfirmed or biased sources Chantreau devised a system of marking suspicious data with the symbol "+," leaving the reader to consider its veracity himself.[79]

Another feature of Chantreau's *Science de l'Histoire*, which he claimed distinguished it from other chronologies, was the way he treated the history of peace by putting information about all European peace treaties from the twelfth century to the Treaty of Amiens into tabular form for easy comprehension. Formerly, he said, these occupied entire volumes or chapters in diplomatic treatises instead of the page or half–page he used to show which powers made each peace and what its terms were.[80]

Chantreau followed the practice of other Imperial historians who sometimes included lists of the most famous people of each period in their chronologies, but with a difference—he separated political figures from literary ones. Thus he made one list for rulers, generals, and statesmen with a brief note containing "the judgment of posterity" on these persons, and another list of philosophers, historians, writers, jurists, mathematicians, and artists followed by what had earned them their fame. Moreover, within each of the two major lists each group was separated from the others by period to enable the student of history to decide

which era furnished the greatest number of historians or philosophers, or which did best in the arts.[81]

In the main body of volume one of the *Science de l'Histoire*,
Chantreau organized the chronology of modern history in three
main columns: at the left appears the year, while in the middle
are the principal facts, with the sources for the study of each
epoch at the right. Most of the information given in the "facts"
column concerns political, military, or economic history. This is
followed by the names of the famous people, as mentioned before;
however, Chantreau actually included lists of famous women,
too. Some interesting snatches of *petite histoire* are interspersed
among more arid facts. For instance, on the reign of Henry IV,
Ravaillac and the twelve years' truce are mentioned, as might be
expected; but Chantreau also noted that during the unusually
cold winter of 1608–9 Henry IV issued an ordinance compelling
the theaters of Paris to start performances promptly at two o'clock
so the citizens could go home at four–thirty before the, then,
unlighted, icy streets grew dark.[82] In his list of notable women of
the period 1688 to 1748 Chantreau inserted a comment for
teachers to use to break up the monotony of teaching chronology;
of Madame de Maintenon he observed that she was "at first
mistress, afterwards, wife of Louis XIV, when he began no longer
to be Louis the Great; mentioned in the history of this prince less
for her fortune than because she made him choose Chamillart for
minister, and Marsin for general; that she had Catinat dismissed
and Vendôme disgraced, that she planned the revocation of the
Edict of Nantes with the Jesuit La Chaise; but excused for all
these faults because she founded St. Cyr, a praiseworthy institution, which ought to earn her the indulgence of posterity."[83]

The remaining two volumes of the *Science de l'Histoire* were
not about history at all, but about European, and Asian, and
American geography, respectively. The second volume was
preceded by a notice that the councilor of state charged with the
direction of surveillance of public instruction had ordered on 2
Pluviose, year XII, that this book be put on reserve at the Bibliothèque des Lycées as one of the works "most useful to public
instruction,"[84] in spite of the fact that many people thought his

geography contained errors. Finally, at the end of the third volume there were four maps, one each of North America, South America, Africa, and Asia, to be used in mastering the science of history.

Chantreau's next–to–last book was a textbook on military history, which he fittingly wrote while he taught at the Ecole Spéciale Impériale Militaire at Fontainebleau. It gave some indication of what attitudes teachers at the school had about the goals of their instruction and what values they were trying to instill in their pupils. Clearly, as Chantreau perceived it, military history was multifariously didactic about such things as the moral virtues of good officers; the methods of great commanders; the conduct of battles and sieges, marches, and prudent retreats, successful ambushes and the precautions taken to prevent being taken by surprise; and the causes, both real and presumed, of the revolutions of states. By reading military history cadets would be stimulated to emulate those truly great commanders who knew never to take credit for themselves for glorious deeds achieved only by the genius of their subordinates or to act unjustly toward their enemies. In addition, by reading military history the young-sters would learn to set examples of emotional control and depri-vation when circumstances warranted, in order to merit the confidence of the troops and the gratitude of their compatriots.[86] The main body of Chantreau's 700–page military history text-book was not really a chronology. Instead, it was arranged topically and included short histoires of conscription, foraging, military pay systems and weapons, with diagrams appropriately placed.

Chantreau ended his career by writing a two–volume chrono-logy of French history,[87] presumably for use at Saint-Cyr, where he was teaching in 1808. In many ways this work, which he dedicated to Fourcroy, is typical of Sérieys' or other Imperial historians' textbooks; however, a careful reading of it reveals certain distinctive qualities that were more marked in Chantreau's thinking and that his other works also display. As usual, his introduction indicated his sources and predecessors—especially Velly and his continuators, Hénault and his own contemporary Anquetil.[88] The contents were divided into at least six major

sections; the principal political, civil, and military events; peace
treaties and commercial treaties with other nations; laws, monuments, discoveries, and the like; a *notice* on the Germanic
Confederation; biographical tables listing famous men of letters,
the arts, the military, diplomacy, and law; and, finally, a map
showing the growth of the city of Paris from Caesar's time to
Napoleon's. Thus, Chantreau incorporated some of the materials
from his *Science de l'Histoire* into this smaller textbook.

The first volume of chronology, which went as far as the year
1715, contains some curious historical ideas. For instance, it said
that King Pharamond established his residence at Heinsberg, six
leagues north of Aix-la-Chapelle, thirteen southeast of Tolbiac,
and thirteen southwest of Tongres; while Clodion resided at
Amiens about the year 438, Childeric at Tournay, and Clovis was
the first king to move into Paris in 509.[89] There was also a two-
page list of all the monuments, bridges, and buildings erected
during the Napoleonic era. Further along was a chart showing
the value of money since the sixth century.[90] The medieval
Emperor Charlemagne was singled out for occupying himself
with public instruction,[91] and subsequently, Chantreau pointed
out that Jacques-Auguste de Thou was a great historian during
the French Renaissance.[92] The biographical section on the kings
of France closed with three pages on Napoleon's family, thus
bringing it completely up to date.[93] Among those whom he listed
as the greatest living historians were five men—Hubert-Pascal
Ameilhon, an able continuator; Pierre-Charles Lévesque, a
member of the Institut who wrote his principal work on the history
of Russia; Christophe-Guillaume Koch, another *instituteur* who
wrote an *abrégé* of peace treaties since the Treaty of Westphalia;
Joseph Servan, a former general and minister, who produced a
history of the Gauls and another of the French military campaigns
in Italy; and Lacretelle the Younger because of his books on the
Legislative Assembly, Convention, and Directory.[94] Another fact
Chantreau mentioned in this first volume is that Madame de
Genlis worked harder on education than any woman in France.[95]
Thus, Chantreau managed to pack many ideas into the first
volume of nearly five hundred pages.

The second volume, covering the years 1715 to 1808, contained over seven hundred pages. It was mostly a chronology describing such things as the first balloon ascension in November, 1783, at the *château royal de la Muette*; the Diamond Necklace Affair of 1786; Chappe's telegraph of 1791; the reorganization of the Institut in 1803, and the fact that the Emperor belonged to the First Class; the organization of the Ecole Speciale Militaire at Fontainebleau in 1803; Guyton-Morveau's discovery of disinfectant for hospitals in 1804; and also that Napoleon and Josephine were crowned at Notre-Dame "by the hands of Pope Pius VII" that same year.[96] The chronology was followed by a three–page alphabetized bibilography of the sources used in the entire work.[97] This, in turn, was followed by François de Neufchâteau's long ode on the four dynasties of France.[98] To his benefactor's poem Chantreau appended a note on how to use it in teaching pupils history, just as Mezerai had done with his poem "Avant Clovis."[99] Finally, pasted to the inside of the back cover was a large fold–out map of Paris. Thus, in spite of its being another chronology, Chantreau's last book showed his particular interests, his interpretation of events, and his loyalty to the regime, as well as his gratitude for patronage. The publication of this *Histoire de France* completed Chantreau's voluminous legacy to the Imperial educational system and historical studies.

Chantreau firmly believed that history is a serious science. He insisted that scientific methods should be followed throughout its teaching–learning process. He placed special emphasis on both careful historical methods and the study of historiography, which included keeping abreast of his colleagues' latest works. His development of new improved instructional materials–such as maps, colored charts, textbooks, teachers' manuals, guides to chronologies with lesson enrichment materials, and poems with teaching suggestions–shows his preoccupation with the idea of using scientific teaching techniques.

Other aspects about his brand of scientific history are also strikingly modern. To him, the scope of history included everything right up to current events, with special emphasis placed upon what is relevant to students. Although history could be

learned chronologically certain themes or topics were also important to him, such as military history, revolution, peace studies,
women's history, and science and technology. Furthermore, he
expended a great deal of time rationalizing the desired government support of his profession by using all the latest arguments
about the social value of the study of history and the search for
truth and justice.

In the end, Chantreau published and perished. The vindica-
tion of his life's work occurred when Napoleon incorporated
many of his ideas into the plans for the Imperial University,
where today the chairs are held by "scientific" historians whose
writing fills the *Annales . . .* of history.

Pierre-Edouard Lemontey (1762–1826) was another of Napoleon's historians; however, in contrast to Chantreau, whose career
was ended by his death in the opening years of the First Empire,
Lemontey's career blossomed much later. In fact, Lemontey
received much less publicity than Lacretelle during the Empire
and consequently fewer details are known about his life prior to
the Bourbon Restoration. Like Lacretelle, Lemontey began his
career as a lawyer. In 1789, he became the prosecutor for the
Commune of Lyon but he expatriated in 1792 and lived in Switzerland.[100] With the advent of the Empire Lemontey was given
the position of jurisconsult in the administration of the *Droits
réunis*. When Napoleon reorganized the ministry of general police
in 1804, he made Lemontey the chief censor of the theaters,[101] a
position he continued to hold until at least 1810, when his annual
salary was set at 1,200 francs.[102] In 1806, Napoleon invited him to
continue Abbé Millot's *Eléments de l'histoire de France* but the
other censors—Joseph Chénier and Lacretelle the Younger—
composed it instead.[103] Then, in 1808, Napoleon gave Lemontey
a pension to write a history of France since the death of Louis XVI
that would show the decadence of the Bourbons in contrast to the
more progressive Fourth Dynasty. The Emperor gave Lemontey
permission to do his research for this book in the secret archives
of the realm and the ministry of foreign affairs. Lemontey became
so engrossed in the task of writing a history worthy of Napoleon

that he was still at work when the events of 1814 ended the Empire. Lemontey published the first fruits of his meticulous research—the introduction—in 1818. Two subsequent volumes on the regency and minority of Louis XV appeared in 1832.[104] Thus, Lemontey's historical writing obviously had no influence on the mentality or historical consciousness of young people or adults during the First Empire. Instead, he was known as the most accomodating Imperial censor.

However, the history that Lemontey finally produced was a masterpiece of which Napoleon would have been proud. It was based on original documents that hitherto were unused. Lemontey broke with the eighteenth–century tradition of writing *á la Pompadour* by making Louis XIV and the Bourbons responsible for bringing on the Revolution; and while this was almost the interpretation that Alexis de Tocqueville later developed,[105] it was also the one that Napoleon had hired Lemontey to write, in 1808. Significantly, in a letter to his friend Pierre-Louis Roederer written in 1820, Lemontey showed that he shared Napoleon's idea that well–written history was the "new history" that was useful, accurate, and critical.

It is apparent that Napoleon's historians were dissimilar in many ways yet each made his contribution to the development of historical studies in nineteenth–century France by providing models for later writers to copy or to improve upon. Lenoir's work made many people more aware of the importance of monuments as historical evidence, while his museum stirred the imagination of the educated people of all ages and nationalities who visited it. Antoine Sérieys turned out more history books than anyone else in Napoleonic France and most of these were read or memorized by youngsters during the Empire and subsequently. Lacretelle the Younger was a precursor of the historical giants of his century. He influenced the university students whom he taught was well as his reading public with accounts of all the interesting events he had witnessed during his long life. Chantreau helped to revive the scientific methodology and historicism of sixteenth–century French historians, thus popularizing the

idea that history is a science based upon facts; he insisted upon
the necessity of teaching history, especially French history, in
the new schools. Finally, Lemontey carried out Napoleon's idea
of the new history during the Restoration. The Emperor provided jobs for talented men, notably as museum curators, censors,
and teachers. Those men who had posts teaching history in the
Imperial University spent much of their time writing textbooks;
in fact, a correlation between their promotions to new teaching
positions and the appearance of their published works seems to
exist, indicating that promotion was the reward for significant
publications. Furthermore, in his patronage system, the Emperor
apparently disregarded any criticism of his historians' works by
others, as the cases of Sérieys and Chantreau indicate.

Overall, this examination of representative Imperial historians
provides a glimpse into the intellectual life of the period from a
perspective below that of the Emperor's, as well as a basis with
which to compare and relate the Emperor's own ideas about history. The fact that some of these historians' careers commenced
prior to the Napoleonic era, even prior to the outbreak of the
Revolution, and continued into the Empire and beyond points
out the essential unity of the intellectual history of the entire
period—Revolution, Consulate, and Empire. In the case of historical studies it appears that Napoleon assimilated many of the
ideas of Imperial historians who, in some instances, had taken
them from the existing discipline, which had roots deep in the
French past. On the other hand, the works of other Imperial
Historians and the timing of the publication of their ideas suggest
that unless it was simple coincidence, the Emperor or the pros-
pect of patronage led them to share his ideas at a given moment.
Regardless of whether it was Imperial historians or the Emperor
who took the lead in formulating the dogma of historical studies,
the genius of Napoleon and his historians lies in the fact that
together they formed part of the continuum of thinkers who
arrived at a consensus about the historical discipline that eventually came to be considered "modern" and is still very much
alive today. Imperial historians also attempted to reconcile "factual science" with "propaganda" favoring the regime, a sensitive

issue wherever scholars are solely dependent upon government subsidization of their teaching and research and whenever the publishing trade is restricted by censorship.

Historical Production Under the Empire

We have seen that Napoleon tried to make history an important part of the curriculum in the Imperial schools and how he patronized the historical field in general. But what were the characteristics of historical writing of the period? Existing descriptions of Imperial history books were written, for the most part, from a negative viewpoint; that is, they used Napoleon's correspondence and other official documents, which emphasized the Emperor's censorship policy regarding history books. They reached conclusions about the historical production of the era not from an examination of actually published works, but by making inferences from those that were repressed. A more positive approach to this subject may be made by examining the historical works that did appear. By this means conclusions may be reached about the quantity and quality of the history that was written and about most of the authors, how they perceived the process of history, what they wrote about, and how they interpreted certain historical events.

Napoleon paved the way for more scholarly research when he became interested in reorganizing the Imperial archives and expanding the holdings of the national library. In 1805 he expressly ordered the minister of interior to augment the national library's collection with works published since 1785 that it lacked. At the same time, he also arranged for the exchange of duplicate copies of old or newer books with other libraries so that the Bibliothèque Impériale would contain a copy of every book existing in France.[1] Five years later in 1810, the Emperor decided to pool all documents regardless of subject from the reign of Louis XIV or earlier in the general archives. Within fifty years, he decided, all the papers from Louis XV's and Louis XVI's reigns would be put into the national archives; meanwhile, they would be reserved so that they could be consulted in the conduct of foreign affairs.[2] The following year, the Institut Impérial published a systematic guide to the Archives of the Empire,[3] which further facilitated scholarly research, especially for historians. Moreover, throughout the Napoleonic era the *Journal général de la littérature de France* contained notices of new manuscripts, which scholars could use, as they arrived at the Bibliothèque Nationale.

The Volume of Historical Writing

Some idea of how much history was actually published during the Empire can be had by examining André Monglond's bibliography *La France révolutionnaire et impériale*, which attempts to list all books written during this period. Between the years 1803 and 1812 more than seven hundred books appeared that could be classified as some type of historical work. If memoirs and letters of historical interest are included, about a thousand history books on all subjects were published during the Empire. These ranged in length from short pamphlets to sizable multivolume works, some of which went through several editions.

Another indication of the sheer volume of writing is found in archival documents for the years 1811 and 1812, which summarized statistics on all the books deposited with the Direction de l'Imprimerie. During the year 1811, 118 works consisting of 166 volumes were received and these editions were printed on 3,665,000 *feuilles* of paper. Also 115 works on education were accounted for; how many of those were history texts is impossible to judge since they are not categorized, nor are their titles given. Other information is given about the monetary value of the 118 histories (all presumably in francs): the paper for their printing cost 73,000, the cost of printing itself was 89,700, and their sale value was 582,000. The following year, 1812, 141 histories were published employing 3,332,000 *feuilles* of paper.[4]

There is a problem of interpretation regarding the volume represented by these statistics because of the use of the word *feuille* in the documents. Books were not printed on cut pages but on printer's sheets, which were printed on both front and back with usually four, eight, or sixteen pages before being folded, bound, and cut. If these figures for *feuille* mean printer's sheets rather than individual books pages, the total number of book pages of history published in 1811 would be approximately 16 x 3,665,000 or 58,640,000 pages. Correspondingly, the total for 1812 would be over 53 million pages—a significant amount indeed.[5]

Aside from the volume of scholarship, Imperial historians liked to write on a wide range of topics. While perhaps two hundred books were written on various aspects of ancient history, there were about four times as many histories published on other subjects. There were nearly as many works written on the Empire and Napoleon as on ancient history. The French Revolution, another popular topic, was the subject of more than seventy books. About three dozen histories of France and two dozen world histories were also published during the Empire, but not all of these were composed recently. The fact that about seventy books were written about persons other than the Emperor should dispel the myth that he permitted historians to write only about himself. Among these, several were on the reigns of Louis XVI, Louis XIV, Charlemagne, and Henri IV. A noticeable number of histories was written about the Celts and the Gauls and at least thirty works were devoted to ancient relics, buildings, medals, and coins.[6]

As in the case of Imperial history textbooks, historical works had several types of formats. Some were chronologies, annals, or books of facts while others were translations of classical Greek and Latin authors as well as of modern European writers. Collections of documents, dissertations, observations, memoirs, and anecdotes were also published along with what might be termed ordinary narrative histories. Another popular way to organize an historical work was in the form of a parallel between two or three great figures of history, such as Caesar, Charlemagne, and Napoleon. Biography was also a popular form.

The authors of Imperial histories were an interesting assortment of people that included some who were no longer living. Editors reprinted new editions of the works of classical authors and of such historians, who were popular in the eighteenth century, as Rollin, Velly, Voltaire, Robertson, Gibbon, and Bossuet. Among the works of historians actually contemporary with the Empire were those of professional historians, many of whom were members of the Institut, like Brial who continued the *Historiens des Gauls* and Pastoret who worked on the *Ordonnances des rois de France.*[7] Members of the faculty of the Imperial University also published; among these were Charles Lacretelle, François Guizot, and Antoine Sérieys. Other Imperial historians were really journalists or poets who occasionally dabbled in history, especially that of the current regime. Many Imperial history books were written by officials who were on the government payroll; some examples of these bureaucrats were the censors, mayors of cities, and the architects of public monuments. Officers in the Grande Armée sometimes described the battles in which they participated and also wrote more general history of warfare. Other histories were written by priests or retired persons who had been unemployed since the Revolution robbed them of important positions in the Old Regime. Not all Imperial histories, however, bore the name of an author. There probably are two explanations for this: either the contents were "subversive," or the government commissioned them to be written for use as propaganda.

The Purpose of History

According to most Imperial history books the purpose of writing history was two-fold: to teach useful lessons to the present generation and to create monuments that would enable future generations to appreciate the past. Especially heavy emphasis was placed on the latter. For example, in 1810, one Imperial historian commented in the introduction to a five–volume work on the history of France: "Happy the historian whose knowledge and genius will call him to the honor of raising a monument which transmits to future centuries our great destinies."[8]

Many other historians discussed in great detail the didactic purpose of history in a manner reminiscent of eighteenth–century historians. In an 1802 manual, Hubert Wandelcourt developed his ideas on the lessons all persons regardless of sex, age, religion, or nationality might derive from the study of history. The law-maker, he said specifically, learns the laws that governed men and the spirit behind their creation, as well as the evil they pre-vented. The statesman learns about the politics of empires and what made some of them rise and others fall. The warrior learns courage and gains experience from warriors of previous centuries and other nations. By studying antiquity the orator learns facts that he can use to make the truth interesting and to move his audiences. And while the sage fortifies his soul from great histor-ical examples, the ordinary citizen is encouraged to practice social virtues. The religious man sees on every page the traces of the Providence that governs the world: he sees that God "grants sceptres and crowns; that he pulls down some, that he raises up others; that he holds in his hands recompenses for the good, chas-tisement for the wicked, and that he makes all the rascals of the earth drink sooner or later from this mysterious cup full of the wine of justice." The man, subject to fits of anger, will learn self-control when he sees in history all the furious passions that left in their wake all sorts of bloody horrors such as war, revolution, vengeance, parricide, and the destruction of empires. The lazy person will see how idleness and effeminacy caused the once–glorious Roman Empire to decay into a servile state. Finally and most important of all, Wandelcourt said, history teaches man to be "good, affable, generous, compassionate, master of his pas-sions."[9] Subsequently, other Imperial historians expressed them-selves in like manner, although in much less detail. M.-A Moithey wrote in his preface that if the study of history is useful to rulers, it is no less useful to ordinary people because it is the best moral code.[10] Similarly, Christophe-Guillaume Koch, a member of the Institut wrote, in 1807, that history augments our own experience by adding that of other men of other centuries, thereby ridding us of acquired prejudices.[11] These examples indicate that Imper-ial historians drew lessons applicable to their own times from their study of the past; they agreed with the eighteenth–century idea of history as philosophy teaching by example.

Historical Methods

In general, Imperial historians were less certain about the definition of history than they were about the purpose of writing it but all their ideas were not entirely compatible. First of all, many historians maintained that history is a science based upon facts and the only difference between it and the physical sciences is that "in history the facts no longer exist; they are dead, and they cannot be resuscitated before the spectator, nor be confronted for testimony."[12] This meant that it must be written scientifically—in a disinterested, impartial manner—in order to present the truth about historical events. Such writers naturally viewed history, chronology, and geography as inseparable fields of unembellished facts. In order to prove the veracity of their accounts they frequently footnoted their work and attached *pièces justificatives*.[13] The number of histories that were really dictionaries or indexes of facts attests to this kind of thinking; notable examples of these were Gillot's *Dictionnaire des Constitutions de l'Empire français et du royaume d'Italie*;[14] Saint-Genois' *Monumens anciens*, which contained lists of feudal proprietorships;[15] a work by De-La-Varenne that contained alphabetical lists of the people killed in the prisons of Paris early in September, 1792, and of those who were in any way responsible for the September massacres;[16] and finally, Pierre-Augustin Barbey-Duquil's *Le Tems ses Evénemens et Morts de marques, depuis l'Année 1784 jusqu'en l'Année 1805*, which contained such basic information about the past as weather reports.[17]

In the lectures he delivered at the Ecole Normale, Charles Volney argued that in the literal sense the word *history* meant not the facts themselves, but research or inquiry after facts. He explained that this was the modest view held by Herodotus and the ancients. Only among the moderns did the foolhardy pretension develop that positive truth about the past could be discovered. However, Volney said that the antique idea—that history is by definition a thorough inquiry after facts—recently came into vogue once again.[18]

In contrast, others emphasized the role of the historian as that

of a judge whose work should criticize the past, the work of previous writers, and historical sources. Continuing in this spirit, R.
De Beaunoir and A. H. Dampmartin wrote that historians should
embellish their accounts to make scenes more real.[19] Then, they
went on to differentiate between the historian and the annalist.
While the latter ought to record facts, only about events he personally witnessed, the historian never should be a contemporary.[20] Obviously, Imperial historians who agreed with these men
could not agree with those who believed that history must simply
be facts, or a search for facts whether recent or long ago, that
leaves the interpretation of events and any embellishment to the
reader's discretion.

   Some historians were sophisticated enough to be able to
reconcile most of these tendencies as reasonably as Volney. He
allowed that while history is an inquiry after facts, the historian
must impartially judge both the reliability of facts as well as their
source as they are presented. The historian's approach must be
analogous to the behavior of a judge in a court of law.[21] After
weighing historical evidence the historian as judge, however, has
to decide how credulous to be because he could believe everything, or nothing, or take a middle position. In considering this
problem Volney decided that the extremes were undesirable:
"pyrrhonism is the feeble ignorance which never judges; and
fanaticism is robust ignorance which always judges." Therefore,
he opted for a happy median: examining doubt would lead cir-
cumspectly to tentative conclusions, which could be redressed if
new proofs were uncovered.[22] Thus, Volney advocated judicious-
ness, something that François Guizot also cautioned in the opening address of his modern history course: "Let us therefore, keep
from thinking that history is really the picture of the past: the
world is too vast, the night of time too obscure and man too feeble
for this picture ever to be complete and faithful."[23] In other
words, "history must be studied with reasoned skepticism."[24]

   That there were indeed in practice two distinct manners of
writing history became clear to Imperial historians themselves
during the debates held by the jury and the Third Class of the
Institut when they chose the Decennial Prize winners. Gaëtan

de Raxis de Flassan, one of the five living authors who competed with the dead for the prize, wrote a scathing denunciation of those authors, whom he called "antihistorians"—those who failed to use their cold reason in examining facts as did de Thou, Daniel, Velly, Gaillard, Millot, and Ameilhon.[25] He maintained that this sect, which formerly had been ridiculed, had begun to rally since the Revolution. He scorned their practices of omitting preliminary remarks and all references to sources and of being inexact about chronology. In particular, he castigated them for using a conventional jargon that made them sound more like poets, painters, novelists, and sculptors than historians; instead of being preoccupied with truth, reason, and stylistic clarity, these fakers spoke of fiction, drama, and illumination.[26] Furthermore, Flassan classified Rulhière, who incidentally was adjudged the winner by the *instituteurs*, among the sect of antihistorians because he made false judgments, arranged his material poorly, and failed to cite his sources.[27]

Further evidence of the trend toward the popularization of a new kind of history is found in an anonymous satire on the "Nouvelle Méthode, pour traiter l'Histoire à la Moderne," which was published in France in 1803. In this piece the author used irony to instruct his readers on how to be successful historians. First of all, he urged, do not fail to write a long preface replete with some relevant and much irrelevant material. Use every occasion to praise Tacitus without going into detail, lest your readers realize that you are totally ignorant of his writings. Before turning to the subject of your book, be sure to affirm your love of the truth although this will make boring reading. Next, find any kind of reason to reject all the authentic memoirs of longstanding on your subject. In order to offer something new take a revisionist approach and write a book proving how badly England was governed by Queen Elizabeth, or that Socrates lacked character, that the Christian martyrs were faithless, that the Protestant Reformers were impious and insincere, that Cromwell was cowardly, or that Cicero disregarded the law. To ornament your history, digress freely; by this means, it is possible to extend a book to folio size when there is really only enough material for an octavo. For

example, in a work on Alexander the Great, a pregnant possibility
for a digression would be to explore what might have happened
had Alexander created his empire in the West and fought a battle
with the Duke of Marlborough. Use erudition in your harangues
because it is unimportant that educated speech issues from the
mouths of the ignorant masses, as long as readers are impressed
by the author's powers of oratory. Finally, to insure your success,
complete your work by inserting numerous scandalous insinua-
tions, criticism of the government, and railleries of religion.[28]
Thus, humorous as well as sober attempts were made by critical
historians to improve the writing of history.

Regardless of whether Imperial historians defined history as
facts or judgment, or both, many of them did use their judgment
to write the present into the past. Sometimes they did so by studying history backward, as Montesquieu had advocated; that is,
they tried to judge the causes of events by first examining their
results or to explain the past as Volney suggested by making analogies with more recent events. Some examples of their line of
reasoning should clarify the idea. For instance, in 1812, Professor N. E. Lemaire of the Faculty of Letters at the Academy of
Paris published a work entitled *Virgile expliqué par le Siècle de
Napoléon*. On another occasion, Maurice Rivoire treated Julius
Caesar as the "Bonaparte of the Romans."[29] As we have seen, this
tendency also carried over into some history textbooks that were
organized with volumes of current history preceding those on
ancient history.[30]

Still another way Imperial historians exercised their judgment
was in the critical use of sources. Some never bothered to cate-
gorize the sources they used; however, the illustrious Christophe-
Guillaume Koch did some thinking about this problem and concluded that there are two kinds of testimony: (1) public documents
and monuments such as medals, inscriptions, treaties, and char-
ters, and (2) the private works of either contemporary or non–
contempory historians or writers.[31] Writing in 1807, Koch went
on to lay down in detail some rules that he felt should guide
historians in choosing their sources. First of all, he believed that
reliable history should always be based upon public documents

and that these took priority over any privately written accounts. Whenever official documents are verified by the testimony of contemporary writers, decisive proof exists. Moreover, the testimony of a contemporary is preferable to second–hand information. If, however, no contemporary writers mention an event, more recent accounts should be regarded as suspect. As for documentation, Koch insisted that historians must list their sources of information. In writing history the able historian must be aware of the prejudices of the authors he uses and the conditions under which each one wrote. Also, authors who had free access to archives ought to be preferred to those who did not. Because the author of this statement was an important public figure his viewpoint may possibly be regarded as representative, at least of some of those historians who belonged to the Institut; at any rate, the Council of the Imperial University eventually adopted Koch's *Tableau des Révolutions de l'Europe* for use in *lycées*.[32]

Not all historians agreed with Koch. Volney divided his authorities into four main classes of historians according to his perception of their reliability: "(1) actual participants, (2) witnesses, (3) interviewers of witnesses, (4) those who relied on hearsay or traditions." He noted that testimony passed from mouth to mouth was invariably falsified and that history rooted in peoples' traditions always had a character related to the degree of ignorance of that civilization. Therefore, he advised caution in believing stories about events that occurred before the invention of printing, which, of course, had tremendous import for the development of historical writing.[33] Volney was also shrewd enough to realize that while the historical authority who personally participates in an event and records his own experiences is usually the most reliable source, once others use his account they read into it whatever they want to, according to their own propensities.[34]

Although other historians did not discuss rules of criticism, many were actually quite critical in their use of sources. François Guizot was adamant about this: "The study of history in order to be done productively, requires a knowledge of men, a solid judgment, and a critical mind."[35] Nor did he hide the fact that

existing works were imperfect: "There is almost no history book
in which a careful examination would not cause the discovery of a
crowd of errors, of false judgments, or risky conjectures, and
perhaps the most part of our ideas on this subject would not stand
up under such an examination."[36] What Guizot advocated was
practiced by J. B. M. Hetzrodt,[37] Baron Silvestre de Sacy,[38] and
Gabriel-Henri Gaillard. The latter published two books that were
outstanding critical works. Gaillard's *Observations sur l'Histoire
de France de Messieurs Velly, Villaret et Garnier* was a three-
volume work consisting of paragraphs excerpted from the works
of famous historians followed by critical remarks and clarifying
information about each excerpt.[39] Another of Gaillard's books,
Histoire de l'Espagne, contained a 37–page analysis of two un-
published manuscripts from the Bibliothèque du roi that told
about the French Captain Gourgues' reprisals for the Spanish
massacre of the French colonists in Florida in 1565.[40] When
Barillet wrote *Recherches historiques sur le Temple*, in addition
to reading all the secondary accounts and comparing and discussing them, he also consulted the letters-patent of the kings,
compilations of the privileges of the order, the civil parish register,
and various manuscripts besides interviewing former inmates of
the prison and other knowledgeable persons.[41] Clearly, Imperial
historians were rather sophisticated in their use of sources.

Philosophies of History

Another way historians exercised critical judgment was the manner in which they interpreted the historical process as a whole.
Not all Napoleonic writers were in agreement, but one idea of
history then in vogue was related to the concept of world history
as a series of ongoing revolutions. Even authors who studied
natural history described the prehistoric period when water
covered the earth's surface as a series of revolutions.[42] The illustrious Koch wrote a *Tableau des Révolutions de l'Europe depuis
le Bouleversement de l'Empire romain en Occident, jusqu'à nos
jours*,[43] which was published in 1807. Other authors said that the
first revolution in French history occurred during the reign of
Childeric III, the last king of the First Race.[44] When P. Labouli-

nière decided to compete for the Decennial Prize offered by the Emperor he wrote a history of France and Europe in which he argued that the same kind of fixed laws that control the tides also govern political revolutions, although the latter are more complicated. Historians call epochs in which these aberrations cause violent upheavals "revolutions."[45] Subsequently, Guizot also wrote in the *Annales de l'éducation* that history should be studied by periods that are defined by the revolutions that have shaken the ideas of men, the social order, and manners.[46] The impact of the French revolutionary experience was evident in the interpretation which some Imperial historians gave to history, as expressed in both books and periodicals.

Other popular historical interpretations were the cyclical and the great–man theories. Some idea of how these were developed by Imperial historians may be gained from V. D. Musset-Pathay's work of 1807, *Recherches historiques sur le cardinal de Retz*, in which he argued that the history of nations resembles the lives of individuals who are born, begin to develop, increase in abilities and extend their influence, conquer others, and then gradually become feeble and pass away.[47] Hence, historians who had personally experienced living through the various phases of the French Revolution readily saw all of history going through similar cycles.

Belief in the great–man theory was especially apparent in Imperial history books. And no wonder! Napoleon was the obvious exemplar. It was widely held that the study of certain great historical figures was even more interesting than national history because the people identify with their leader and take on his characteristic virtues and vices. Musset-Pathay thus explained why he thought historians almost involuntarily focus on the great man in history.[48] Portalis *fils* wrote an eloquent and much-acclaimed essay on this subject in 1800, in which he expressed his belief that the genius of a single person can become that of an entire nation and conversely, that the genius of the nation exerts an influence upon the body and soul of the great man. As he assesses the hero in history, the historian must remember that "one man is never an isolated being."[49] The hero cannot be con-

sidered apart from his culture. Portalis *fils* also went on to describe
who the great man in history is and how he functions. He saw him
as one who is both contemplative and effective, completing in a
moment what mediocre men fail to achieve in a century because
of the tremendous energy of his will. His eagerness to fulfill his
destiny raises his soul beyond the reach of misfortune while the
obstacles he encounters only serve to strengthen his resolve.[50] In
1806, Louis Dubroca concluded that even the childhood of great
men differs from that of ordinary mortals and foreshadows their
exceptional careers. Moreover, "nature only produces one of
these phenomena at great periodic intervals. . . ."[51] These historians saw heroes in history during the early Consular period as
well as during the Empire, when the destiny of France and
Europe was in the hands of a man who himself had studied the
heroes of history; he attempted to play that role even after his fall
from power by preparing for his own apotheosis in the historical
writing he produced and by the philosophizing in which he
engaged on Saint Helena. Perhaps contemplation of heroes from
the past filled a psychological need of the present for Napoleon's
disturbed and insecure historians who hoped, as Moithey did, for
a new hero to emerge for the sake of France: "After so many
revolutions, we need a new Charlemagne. . . ."[52]

The Interpretation of French History

Several historians wrote works about the three defunct Dynasties
of French kings; like the authors of textbooks, they were especially
interested in why the dynasties succeeded each other and what
made each legitimate. Regardless of which dynasty they treated,
the same definite viewpoint is apparent in these interpretations:
weak kings who lacked courage were overthrown by popular and
talented men who embodied "the supreme will of the nation."[53]
Both Pepin and Hugh Capet sensed what caused the extinction of
their predecessors' dynasties and they both consciously worked
to mend the political disorders existing in their realms. Consequently, the state developed new vigor and order prevailed once
again.[54] The source of weakness in monarchs was generally
understood to be sweetness, goodness, and piety in their per-

sonalities—something which, for example, kings as remote as the successors of Clovis II had, thereby leading ultimately to their being overthrown by the ambitious Carolingians.[55] But the rulers' early education and advisors often were important causes of dynastic degeneration. Inept or perfidious teachers who perverted their thought processes, dissipated their physical stamina, and separated them from all knowledge of men and the world as children, succeeded in transforming them into "the plaything of those who approached them" in their adulthood.[56] Hence, new dynasties were needed to lead the nation to greatness. The popular will legitimatized the authority of the new strong-man, as it did that of Charles Martel, Hugh Capet, and Napoleon.

Medievalists paid much attention to the question of who was really the founder of the French monarchy. The historian Louis Dubroca said that there were four kings before Clovis but, since they were unable to maintain possession of their territories, he considered Clovis as the actual founder of the First Dynasty. Thus he shared the idea that Pharamond was the first king of France. In his book, moreover, Dubroca supplied a picture of Clovis who, he said, founded the French monarchy in A.D. 486.[57] Gaëtan de Raxis de Flassan agreed that properly speaking Clovis was the founder of the French monarchy, but he believed that Clodion was the first nonmythical king of the Franks because Pharamond was unknown to such ancient writers as Gregory of Tours and Frédégaire the Scholastic.[58]

Although Imperial historians themselves were interested in studying medieval history, some of them thought it could be dangerous for public morality. Charles Volney cautioned against exposing young people to knowledge about this period because it could result in the creation of a destructive, warrior society like that of the Teutons. Nations, he believed, are just as subject to a higher law as are individuals and for neither does might make right. Wolves and tigers, he pointed out, are capable of loving their own kind, but human beings must learn to love their neighbors in other nations, as well as those next door. In the year III Volney had seen children who were accustomed to innocent forms of recreation lanterning cats and guillotining birds in imitation of the revolutionary tribunals and he feared what children who were reared with a knowledge of rapine and carnage might do when they became adults.[59] Thus, he deemed the study of medieval history fit only for persons with characters strong enough to withstand this example of excessive violence and immorality.

The study of the first of the Bourbon kings was a more appropriate subject for young persons. It was part of Napoleon's official policy to revitalize the memory of Henry IV among the French people. Statues were erected in Henry's honor, artists used him as a source of inspiration, and theaters included plays about him in their repertoires. Historians also played a role in this revival.[60] As one writer phrased it, books about the monarch's life molded the reader's heart: "and who would not be moved hearing about the noble deeds of our good Henry!"[61] The assassination of Henry IV was also used as a morality lesson for would-be assassins. In 1813, Madame Guizot published a story about a little boy whose father took him to visit rue de la Féronnerie where Ravaillac had assassinated the king. When the lad passed the scene of the crime, he felt a terrible sadness and chagrin, but his father reminded him that even criminals have some good qualities. There is, he continued, both good and evil in history. In this case, Ravaillac killed Henry IV in good conscience because he thought the king was a Huguenot, although he should have followed the Scriptural command: "Thou shalt not kill." Hence, great evil can sometimes be the result of good intentions when people fail to remember the ultimate basis of morality, as the assassination of the beloved monarch proved.[62]

Most Imperial historians did not write as glowing accounts of the reign of Louis XIV as eighteenth–century writers had. Charles Lacretelle detected both good and evil in the reign of the Sun King. By 1709, he observed, France was in dire circumstances, with both rural and urban areas depopulated as a result of war and the revocation of the Edict of Nantes. When Louis died in 1715, Lacretelle said, it was "after all the prosperities, the long struggles, the splendor, the misery, the meritorious successes and the great mistakes of a sixty–two year reign. . . ."[63] One critic who reviewed his book said that if Lacretelle had provided a more detailed discussion of Louis XIV's reign he would also have found "in the depopulation of France, in the decadence of its commerce and manufacturing, in the exhaustion of its finances, in the poor choice of his ministers and generals, in the revocation of the edict of Nantes, in several ruinous wars, in the immensely lavish taste for buildings of pure luxury, in the baleful influence of an all powerful mistress, the manifest and secret causes which prepared the reverses of the last years of Louis XIV. . . . "[64] Nevertheless, Lacretelle did not fail to realize the significance of the gross insults that were hurled by the people at the king's funeral cortège: "The remains of Louis XIV, insulted in 1715, were exhumed in 1793, with those of all our kings. The monarchy already had received a blow the day when the funeral procession of such a monarch was profaned."[65]

Despite the fact that censors dealt harshly with books written about the last Bourbons,[66] many were published and sold openly. In addition to creating new works on the Bourbon kings, authors of guides for studying history encouraged persons who sought enlightenment to read what were considered to be the best existing books available. For example, in 1803, François Née de la Rochelle encouraged the reading of these older works on the reign of Louis XVI:

Mémoires pour servir à l'Histoire de Louis, Dauphin de France, fils de Louis XV, by Père Griffet (1777).

Vie de Dauphin, Père de Louis XVI, by Abbé Proyart (1782).

Anecdotes du Règne de Louis XVI, compiled by Nougaret (1791).

Louis XV et Louis XVI, by Antoine Fantin-Desodoards (1798).

Histoire du Procès de Louis XVI, or Analyse de toutes les Pièces qui ont servi de base à son Jugement (1793).

Mémoires du Comte de Maurepas, Premier Ministre de Louis XVI, etc. (n.d.).

Histoire Raisonée des Operations Militaires et Politiques de la dernière guerre, by Joly de Saint-Vallier (1784).

Vie de Turgot, Ministre d'Etat sous le Règne de Louis XVI,
by the Marquis de Condorcet (1786).

*Mémoires du Comte de Saint-Germaine, Ministre de la
Guerre sous le Règne de Louis XVI* (1779).

*Correspondance particulière du même Comte de Saint-
Germaine avec M. Paris Duverney* (1790).

And finally in a section on ceremonials, he recommended an
illustrated folio-volume, *Le Sacre et Couronnement de Louis
XVI, fait à Reims, le 11 juin 1775* (1775).[67] Thus, there really was
no wholesale attempt by the censors to curtail the study of the last
Bourbon monarchs. De-La-Varenne understood this when, in
1806, he wrote: "We are no longer in those times of ignorance, of
crime, and of sorrow when the names of the Sovereigns could
only be spoken with horror; and they acknowledge today, fear-
lessly, that the dying royalty still conserves the majestic brilliance
of the setting sun."[68] Even Louis XVI's own translation of Horace
Walpole's manuscript on Richard III, made in 1782, was published
in 1801 and promoted in the journals.[69]

In newly created histories Louis XV and Louis XVI received
the same kind of treatment they did in the textbooks written for
use in Imperial schools. In 1807, Costard wrote a short study of
Louis XV and his court that was supposed to contain heretofore
unknown information about this monarch. What Costard had to
say about Louis XV's personality corresponds with the way Imperial historians interpreted the fall of dynasties in general.
Costard actually made excuses for Louis XV's behavior and
described him as a good soul who unfortunately was corrupted
by his surroundings.[70] He concluded that: "Louis was one of the
examples of the fatality by which, under the best princes, the
people often find themselves capable of evils. He had all the
qualities which in a sovereign serve to do honor to humanity;
good husband, good father, good lover, good friend, full of honor
and probity, Louis XV is credited with being one of the most
honorable men of his realm; he had only one defect, that of being
king."[71] And in Flassan's diplomatic history, published in 1809,
Louis XV was described as having more good qualities than bad

ones. For example, he had a good memory, presence of mind, judgment, and was modest to a fault, but the ill effects of the partition of Poland at the end of his reign overshadowed such accomplishments as the acquisition of Lorraine and Corsica along with the expansion of maritime commerce.[72]

Historians treated Louis XVI's situation somewhat less generously though sympathetically. In 1802, P.C. Lecomte portrayed Louis XVI as virtuous but behaving feebly and wanting in character because he acquiesced to court pressure that ultimately resulted in the state's financial ruin. He began his reign benevolently and ended it abandoned by family, nobility, and clergy. In an effort to please everyone, he drifted among the factions until he became the victim of them all.[73] Subsequent authors emphasized that in addition to lacking all the qualities vital to being a successful ruler, the last Bourbon king also was surrounded by intriguing courtiers and effeminate princes. Bearing these facts in mind, one writer asked: "How could Louis XVI maintain his throne in the bosom of political tempests and of violations of the oath of allegiance made to him?"[74] In fact, another insisted on his utter helplessness: "All causes . . . necessitated a change of regime; it was inevitable. It was necessary, in effect, to cede to the general will, to the most universal impulse which had ever taken place in a great nation."[75] Subsequently, Louis XVI was treated even more sympathetically; by 1810, his experience "proved that goodness, when it is not accompanied by firmness, has more disastrous consequences than vices in a sovereign."[76] Clearly Imperial historians used their independent judgment in their treatment of the Bourbons. They did not condone their reigns; nevertheless, they treated them as fallible human beings who individually deserved compassion, rather than vituperation. A.-H. Dampmartin explained the reason for this reluctance to condemn the Bourbons in his book *La France sous ses rois*, which appeared in 1810. People, he said, are bound to react differently to the demise of a dynasty hundreds of years old; they will respond with feelings ranging from deep regret, fear, or melancholia to reproachfulness and extreme hatred, according to their own characters. Furthermore, Dampmartin stated emphatically, the new sovereign could in no way rely upon the loyalty of those who were most antipathetic to his forerunner.[77] Thus, those who viewed Louis XVI as a human being who suffered great misfortunes were not necessarily guilty of any disloyalty toward the Empire; in fact, they were Napoleon's more trustworthy subjects.

The Interpretation of the Revolutionary Era

General treatments of the French Revolution were a favorite topic of Imperial historians. Such writings, if done impartially, were considered as rendering a public service; they would serve as a mirror for the factious who, it was hoped, would discard their prejudices once they became conscious of them. According to Emmanual Toulongeon, by reading a well–written history of the recent revolution Jacobins could realize that all émigrés did not participate in antirepublican agitation and, likewise, royalists would discover that all patriots were not Jacobins.[78] The author of an anonymous work on the French Revolution, from the death of Louis XVI to Napoleon's coronation, forewarned his readers that he would weigh both the incalculable evils and great patriotic deeds, but in so doing, he would mention only deceased culprits by name since death enlisted them in the domain of history. By abiding by such a rule, the author felt he aided paternal govern-ment in maintaining domestic tranquility.[79] Clearly, the manner in which such historians dealt with the French Revolution con-formed to official censorship policy.

General histories of the French Revolution naturally included a section on Philippe Egalité. Generally, the Red Prince was described as a traitor to his country for promoting the Revolu-tion. Several works explained how the British were really re-sponsible for this event.[80] According to Antoine Sérieys, Pitt planned to take revenge on the French for aiding the English colonists in the American Revolution by hiring Philippe d'Orléans to organize a revolution in France in 1789.[81] On the day of October 5, 1789, men wearing women's clothing stopped some of the women who were doing their marketing and forced them to join the insurrection.[82] As part of this plot Orléans disguised himself and marched in female attire along with the women to

Versailles. When a group of women recognized him, he exhorted them to be patriotic and courageous and to remember that the king and queen, who were inside the château, were the source of all the people's unhappiness.[83] In the minds of Imperial historians such a man, "without liberal ideas, without true patriotism,"[84] deserved to die on the scaffold if for no other reason than the fact that he coldly voted for the death of one of his blood relatives when he should have abstained.[85] As a further indication of his perfidious nature, Philippe Egalité observed his cousin's execution from a cabriolet parked on the pont Louis XVI.[86]

Many plot theorists were convinced that Pitt had indeed been responsible for instigating and continuing the Revolution; however, by 1801 this idea had also become part of a joke about a horse race purportedly held on the Champ de Mars in 1793. At first, the judges refused to award the prize to the victor, due to the fact that the horse had English blood. Immediately, they ordered that since the horse seemed suspect and might be in the pay of Pitt or Cobourg, the rider had to produce certificates of the horse's civil status and of his residency since Bastille Day to prove its nonemigration.[87]

Besides Philippe Egalité and Pitt, Imperial historians detected others as plotters of revolution. Colonel Swan, who had participated in the Boston Tea Party, lived in Paris before and after July 14, 1789. Swan, it was said, invited Thomas Jefferson, the Lameth brothers, and all the young officers who had fought in the American war of independence to dine at his mysterious house in Chaillot where, in the absence of the servants, they magically set up tables that appeared from secret traps. Then they drank fine wines that warmed their spirits until they conjured up plans to usurp the king's prerogatives. It was further theorized that the American ambassador's residence served as a club where the germs of the French Revolution were incubated; therefore, Sérieys concluded that Thomas Jefferson was one of the promoters of republicanism. Such was the role of the Bostonian club and the future president of the United States.[88] If such conspiracy theories seemed incredible, historians reminded their readers that there had to be a special explanation for the coming of the revolution

because while there were abuses in the Old Regime and strong
opposition to these existed, the French monarchy had fewer
vices than any other European government.[89]

Other historians insisted that the French Revolution was
unique precisely because its outbreak was spontaneous. As A.F.
Bertrand de Moleville observed, it probably was the only revolution that had ever broken out without premeditation or without
having any recognized head to its parties. Instead of a plot, he
said, every revolution is caused by the weakness of the government that is overthrown. Another unique feature, according to
Bertrand de Moleville, was that previously the legitimate government was simply replaced by a more despotic one, whereas in
France a series of revolutions, actually five of them, had succeeded each other like a "revolutionary hydra."[90]

In his important multivolume history of the French Revolution, Toulongeon took a somewhat deterministic view of causation by comparing the French Revolution to the Lisbon earth-
quake. He saw both conflagrations as inevitable because their
beginnings were lodged somewhere in the remote past and could
only be conjectured. Such a view refuted the plausibility of the
idea that one man or even a whole party could be held solely
responsible. In accordance with these ideas, Toulongeon looked
far beyond the reign of Louis XIV—to the Renaissance—for the
seeds of the French Revolution.[91]

Other historians saw the revolutionary outburst of republicanism and principles of liberty originating in the Protestant
Reformation. In an essay that was crowned by the Institut,
Charles Villers established a causal relationship between the two
events by pointing out that Protestant ideas were carried to the
English colonies by people fleeing religious persecution. These
ideas of liberty later were carried to France by the French soldiers
who aided the Americans in their war of independence.[92] Another contender for the Institut's prize, Malleville *fils*, saw a different causal relationship between the Reformation and the
French Revolution. In his interpretation, the republican spirit
issuing from the sixteenth–century upheaval was held in check
by Richelieu and Louis XIV but found advocates in the parle-

ments. It continued to be nurtured there until 1788, when it spawned the germ of independence and opposition to the monarchy. As an Imperial reviewer observed of Malleville's essay: "In recognizing that the spirit of republicanism took its source in France from the introduction of the principles of the reformation, the author saw a hidden fire escaping which destroyed the state in 1789."[93] By acclaiming both of these essays the academicians of a government that was officially attached to the Roman Catholic faith acknowledged the effect of Protestant ideas on their national history.

Other authors embraced a more short-ranged view of revolutionary origins. In 1803 Abbé Proyart, a staunch Catholic who was already known for his *Vie du Dauphin, père de Louis XVI*, published a work on the causes of the French Revolution entitled *Louis XVI détrôné avant d'être Roi*. The thesis of this book was that the Revolution was caused by the deeds of philosophic ministers during the reign of Louis XV. In a reviewer's estimation, Proyart attributed nothing to chance and singled out the immediate causes, but beyond everything Proyart saw operating a providence, which linked the morality of a people with the morality of those who govern them.[94] Lecomte, who had a reputation for moderation, believed that the Revolution began in 1771 when the *parlementaires* planned an insurrection.[95] In both of these interpretations revolutionary origins also predated the reign of Louis XVI.

Often Imperial historians attributed the outbreak of the Revolution to more immediate events of Louis XVI's reign. While some writers agreed with Dubroca that his fall from power was caused by the fact that all the factions united momentarily to unseat him,[96] others returned to the theme of the American war. Even before the American Declaration of Independence the French government had clandestinely aided the English colonists. As proof of this, a letter in the archives written by Count Vergennes showed that Caron Beaumarchais shipped them arms, clothing, and munitions and then beginning in May, 1776, the French government supplied direct monetary assistance.[97] On February 6, 1778, Louis XVI committed the fatal blunder, which

was his undoing—signing the treaties of commerce and alliance
with the United States. This set off the chain of events beginning
with the creation of the financial deficit and leading through the
Estates-General to the fall of the monarchy. In other words,
according to Flassan, the American revolutionary war caused
"one of the most terrible catastrophes of which history makes
mention."[98]

In a much lighter vein, Capelle drew attention to another
cause, which the public as well as professional historians noted,
in a story he told that referred to the Diamond Necklace Affair.
"You must write me the history of the French Revolution, said a
publisher to a man of letters; but I would like this history to be
preceded by a tableau of France in 1788 and at the beginning of
1789. —That being the case, responded the author, we will lead
the revolution by the collar."[99] Thus, there was really no general
agreement about whether factionalism, finances and the American Revolution, or the immorality of the court itself had preci-
pitated the end of the *ancien régime*. Nor was there a consensus
about which century since the Renaissance was the actual setting
for the origins of that cataclysmic event.

Some of Napoleon's historians attempted to erase unpleasant
memories of the Revolution. Enough years had elapsed to enable
people to reminisce selectively, blotting out the worst horrors
and laughing about many of the customs that were popular when
they were younger. Thus Jean Pierre Papon dismissed writing
the details of the Reign of Terror: "When the body politic is dead,
what need is there to follow it into the last degrees of putrefaction
. . .?"[100] On the other hand, Capelle tried to help people forget
the baleful events by making them laugh at revolutionary manners and participants, without naming anyone. Hence, he told
about the sign on the door of the headquarters of a revolutionary
committee: "*Tutoiement* is used here: close the door *s'il vous
plaît*."[101] He also jested about the seats in the Convention, saying
that in the countryside the peasants predict the harshness of
winter by observing how high the turkeys perch. Upon seeing
the Convention with the Mountain almost deserted, one villager
was heard to exclaim: "Thank God, it's not going to be a hard

winter!"[102] Usually, however, historians pointed to the excesses of the Revolution and viewed them as a tragedy.

Since Robespierre was dead, historians could freely criticize him, as Lacretelle severely did in his précis of the National Convention. Depicting him as the worst culprit to ever menace France with a reign of destruction, Lacretelle said that his single passion for crime made him so sinister that even his accomplices were unable to fathom his motivation or to distract him from his pursuit of crime.[103] Dubroca mentioned the cruel competition that had ensued among the various parties in the struggle for power as they, in turn, devoured each other over a three–year period, creating such a spectacle that "history will for a long time be fearful of tracing a picture of it."[104] Nevertheless, he went on to trace its worst aspect as being the creation of a societal witch hunt in which everything, including the tear shed in grief at the loss of a friend, became a form of *lese-nation*.[105] But his era of calamities was not without redeeming features because "The Good, in physical and moral nature, only descends upon us from the sky, slowly, little by little." This might have been the end of the nation if virtue had not taken refuge in the French armies, where the first rays of the immense glory of the greatest of the nation's heroes showed forth.[106] After the execution of Robespierre, France began to recover; oh, "What a fine day was the night of 9 Thermidor!"[107] Subsequently, a new government—the Directory—was organized, which was the first to conserve the social order since the creation of the republic.[108]

In general, historians treated the Directory as an unstable period characterized by corruption and anarchy. Capelle, with his usual wit, mocked the elected officials by telling a tale about an offhand remark made to a representative about there being so many scoundrels among them. His answer was that a great state must represent everybody.[109] Lacretelle, however, did not regard the Directory as a whole, but as two distinct periods separated by the 18 Fructidor and ending, naturally, with the 18 Brumaire. During the first part, he said, national glory and domestic peace were normal but the later period was a long progression of misery when "the government operated without finances and almost

without law." France was in "a rather confused state; but it led to
an unhoped for denouement which terminated the revolution
and which brought back laws as well as victories."[110] Meanwhile,
the glory of the generals eclipsed that of the directors, whom the
people did not respect—"five diverse physiognomies, but so
barely salient that they could scarcely distinguish them from each
other."[111] During all of this time, according to Lacretelle, the
monarchy was not forgotten and there was "a vague but constant
need" for its return.[112] D.-F. Donnant, writing in 1811, phrased
this need poetically: "Tired of battling against the tempests, an
entire people about to perish implored a savior. All eyes were
turned toward him, all the voices demanded him and designated
him: his glory and his name passed from hearts to lips; his great
reputation gave birth to the sweetest hopes."[113] These historians
looked for some sort of *deus ex machina* to put an end to a period
of uncertainty.

Napoleon's remarkable return from Egypt in 1799 found its
way into all the history books. As Nicholas Vitron de Saint-Allais
explained in an 1803 work, "The supplications of the French
people carried themselves toward the Orient . . .," to the consciousness of the only man capable of saving the imperilled
republic. He, however, was beyond the normally insurmountable
barrier formed by the immense naval fleets of France's enemies.[114]
But Dubroca intimated in 1806 that whoever sent for Bonaparte
was unknown. Regardless, people would rather believe that their
hero was so touched by the evil events that he was forced to cede
to this overwhelming desire to set them aright.[115] Regardless of
what had made him decide to return at that moment, the political
confusion was about to be ended. "Such was the vow of the
French; it penetrated into the heart of Napoleon, and the 18
Brumaire was resolved."[116]

According to Napoleon's historians the hour of deliverance
arrived on the 18 Brumaire.[117] When cries of "outlaw" were
heard on that day "it seemed like Caesar was in the midst of the
senate which should slay him; one of the generals made a shield
for Napoleon with his body and drew him out of the Council."[118]
The armed forces came into the hall and the representatives of

the people jumped out of the windows in order to allow the good to be accomplished.[119] That evening, the rump of the Five Hundred, consisting of the majority freed from domination by the "impetuous minority," returned with their president leading them and declared that Bonaparte deserved to head the government; from this moment the Revolution was consummated.[120] Such interpretations were obviously meant to bolster the Napoleonic regime.

The creation of the Empire in 1804 was a further stimulus to authors. The coronation ceremony, which was consciously patterned after that of Charlemagne, set the tone. Many thought as Jean-Charles Jumel did that "nature had to repose for ten centuries in order to produce a genius capable of matching and perfecting the work of Charlemagne."[121] As much as historians liked to draw parallels, however, they insisted on Napoleon's unique achievements and on the purity of his private life. Even before the coronation, V.-R. Barbet de Bertrand wrote that Bonaparte was unique because he did in thirty months what it had taken Charlemagne thirty years to accomplish. Also his private life was not analogous because he was a good-hearted "young patriarch" whose character was comparable only to the innocent simplicity of nature, whereas licentiousness, and shameless incestuousness had characterized Charlemagne's household.[122] Likewise, in 1806 Dubroca argued that there really was no comparison between Napoleon and the other founders of French dynasties because he was far superior.[123] The evocation of Charlemagne's memory, therefore, proved favorable to the Emperor Napoleon I.

The creation of the Empire was regarded by historians as abruptly beginning a new era. Dubroca, who developed this idea rather fully, contended that never had any nation exercised its right of sovereignty as freely as did the French when they elevated Napoleon to the position of hereditary Emperor by the plebiscite. The army, all those who had civil careers during the Revolution, the acquirers of parcels of the national domain, the priests of the temples, and all classes of peaceable citizens who wished to consolidate their gains from the Revolution or who were tired of political turmoil heralded the advent of Napoleon. Dubroca concluded that while the Empire insured liberty, it was a "total renewal of things," and "a new era."[124] Similarly, in 1810, Dampmartin described the foundation of the French Empire by making an allusion to the Roman Empire. Rome formerly had been mistress of the world, protector of the feeble, sparer of the vanquished, and conqueror of the mighty. Imperial France assumed this role after fifteen years of revolutionary disorder by returning to the antique bases of social order—religion, heredity, and unity of power.[125] Along these lines historians suggested that the new French Empire, based upon popular sovereignty, was the potential mistress of the world in the age about to unfold.

Why had republicanism failed to take root in France? Historians also worked out the answer to this question on the basis of their knowledge of both ancient and modern history and suggested that monarchical tradition was too strong. They interpreted republicanism as being a fantasy of almost all peoples of the earth who had suffered from abuses of monarchs, but it never endured because people soon realized that they needed a supreme leader to mitigate factionalism. They distinguished between a government that was republican from its origins and one that superseded a monarchical tradition of glory and prosperity. The latter was doomed to failure like a house built on sand because while appearances changed, what was in peoples' hearts remained the same until it finally erupted, leading thereby to a restoration. Such was the case with the thirteen–century–old French monarchy, which rejected the attempted grafting of an alien republican tradition onto its monarchical trunk.[126] In such fashion, Imperial historians brought judgments of current events before their readership.

Summary

In conclusion, an examination of historical works of the Napoleonic era indicates that the quality of historical writing was changing. The Emperor encouraged historians to practice their craft and their production was prodigious, much of it based on meticulous research. Although Imperial historians generally regarded the purpose of history as their predecessors had, they were ambivalent in their precise definition of "history." Some of them adhered to Mably's idea of the historian as judge, while others stressed the need for scientific methodology and complete objectivity. Actually, their works showed a certain amount of both judgment and objectivity. Occasionally, they wrote the present into their interpretations of the past but if they did, they documented it better. They wrote on many topics, including the Bourbons and the French Revolution, and made nearly all of the past seem relevant to current events. The continuity of the historical process thus was often stressed and a liberal bias was apparent among the interpretations Imperial historians gave to events in their national history.

Overall, treatment of the period from 1789 to 1795 seems to be an attempt at accommodation, at healing the cleavages in Imperial society. Several historians believed that a causal relationship existed between the American and French Revolutions, stemming from French economic involvement and ideas about freedom carried back to Europe by returning war veterans. Plot-theorists singled out several individuals as being responsible for fomenting the Revolution; the Freemasons, especially, were frequently blamed for its outbreak.

Treatment of more immediate events, such as the legitimate basis for the establishment of the Empire, is a more markedly blatant attempt to bolster the Napoleonic regime. Paradoxically, the prevalent belief that France ought to return to the popular and natural form of monarchy permeates almost all aspects of the revolutionary historiography of the First Empire. While the historical production of the Napoleonic era reveals an attempt to strive for impartiality, nevertheless, it reveals also the imprint made by the revolutionary experience on the minds of these devotées of Clio. The horror and strain of the Revolution compelled historians to long for the tranquillity now associated with the monarchy. Even under the Consulate and Empire, the movement of thought was toward a restoration and so in advance Napoleon's historians unwittingly signaled the retreat from Waterloo and the necessity of the final abdication.

Conclusion

A study of the historical discipline in Napoleonic France raises the whole question of literary and intellectual activity in an authoritarian state. The natural tendency is to think that such an activity, generally involving freedom of thought and expression, is not possible; however, the examples of the historical writing done in nineteenth–century Russia, or even in France under Louis XIV, suggest that it is. The study just completed also substantiates this.

What Napoleon articulated about his idea of history leaves something to be desired. His ideas certainly were not entirely original or logical. On the sole basis of what he personally said and wrote it could possibly be argued that he viewed history as a science or *per contra* as propaganda; but his plans for putting history into the school-rooms of the Empire indicate that he really was interested only in how it could shape the mentality of his subjects in order to make them more loyal to the regime. In comparison to that of some of his contemporaries Napoleon's talent as an historian was mediocre; certainly, he lacked the objectivity demonstrated by some scholars. Nevertheless, the ambivalence in his thinking and his preoccupation with more pressing matters, in addition to his genuine desire to patronize the arts in imitation of the Bourbons, gave serious scholars the opportunity to pursue their interests in the archives. While the regime intruded into the discipline, it did not trample roughshod on respectable historical production. Moreover, the historically conscious Emperor stimulated historians' imaginations with his exploits and public-work projects. The Empire also provided a period of training for the great French historians of the nineteenth century, such as Michelet, Thierry, Lemontey, and Guizot.

The first Empire thus was an important transitional period in the development of historical scholarship in France during which scholars laid the necessary foundation for subsequent outstanding achievements. The emperor began to reorganize the national libraries and archives. Under his patronage members of the Institut prepared inventories and published catalogues. They also edited important series of documents relating to the history of France. The contests they sponsored were designed to encourage better scholarship among historians in France and in other countries as well. It is noteworthy that history professors holding teaching posts in the Imperial University and at German universities were singled out as representing the finest in scholarly ability. The historical value of ancient monuments, coins, works of art, and other artifacts as evidence of prior customs and civilization became clearer as Napoleon patronized museum collections, notably of French and Egyptian artifacts. In all of these ways Napoleon prepared for the future development of the historical discipline.

Many Imperial historians worked hard to advance historical studies beyond the level of the eighteenth century. They were critical of the research of their forebears and of each other. They had enough faith in themselves and in their fellow men to believe that history could be developed into a scientific discipline—a branch of the social sciences—which would work toward making society better and happier. The content of new historical works written for adult audiences was on a more mature and less propagandistic level than the textbooks designed for children. Regardless of whether they believed that history moved deterministically or was freely turned in certain directions by the efforts of great men, Imperial historians had a vision of the history of France and of the world at large as being part of a great, secular, organic process that progressed in time without ever ending. In other words, they were already historicist in the double sense of the term—from the standpoint of both philosophy and objective method.

NOTES

Preface

1. Père Joseph de Jouvency (1643–1719), a noted Jesuit educator, wrote pedagogical treatises and Latin textbooks, some of which were reprinted during the First Empire.

2. Charles Rollin (1661–1741), illustrious historian, rector of the University of Paris, and son of a tradesman, was known for his Jansenist sympathies for which he lost the privilege of teaching. In the enforced leisure of his later years, he devoted his time to writing. Although his best-known works are his ancient and Roman histories, it is his *Traité des Etudes*, published from 1726 to 1731, that contains his innovative system of education, emphasizing the use of French instead of Latin.

3. Père Clément Buffier (1661–1737), a Jesuit educator born in Poland, published about twenty works that were mostly religion, history, and science. He was best known during the First Empire as a zoologist and for his theories of learning and child psychology.

4. Père Bernard Lamy (1640–1715), an Oratorian, wrote numerous works on teaching reading, science, mathematics, and rhetoric.

5. Louis-Réné de Caradeuc de La Chalotais (1704–85), procurer general of the parlement of Brittany, wrote an important essay on a plan of national education that he wanted to see implemented after the expulsion of the Jesuits.

6. Père Gabriel Daniel (1649–1728), *historiographe de France*, wrote a popular history of the monarchy from the Gauls to Louis XIII's reign.

7. Charles-J.-Fr. Hénault (1685–1770), president of the parlement of Paris and superintendent of the Queen's household, was the compiler of chronologies on French and Spanish and Portuguese history.

8. Abbé Gabriel Bonnet de Mably (1709–85), brother of the philosophe Condillac and canon of the abbey church of Saint-Barbe, was most famous for his history of France. He also wrote observations on the governments of Greece, Rome, Poland, and the United States.

9. Abbé Paul-Fr. Velly's (1709–59) history of France was such an accepted standard that Villaret, Garnier, and Antoine Fantin-Desodoards extended it to fifty-six volumes.

10. Abbé Claude-Fr. -Xavier Millot (1726–85), successively professor of rhetoric at the Jesuit College of Lyon, archbishop of Lyon, and professor of history at the University of Parma, wrote several histories, all of which were reprinted repeatedly.

11. See: Jean Morange and Jean-François Chassaing, *Le Mouvement de réforme de l'enseignement en France 1760–1798* (Paris: Presses Universitaires de France, 1974).

12. Barthélemy-Gabriel Roland d'Erceville (1734–94) was president of the *requêtes* of the parlement of Paris; his *Plan d'Education* was published in 1784.

CHAPTER I

1. His brother Joseph recalled how at school at Ajaccio the class was divided into groups for games with sides representing Romans and Carthaginians. Joseph Bonaparte, *Mémoires et correspondance politique et militaire du roi Joseph*, 1: 40–41. Cited by

Harold T. Parker, "The Formation of Napoleon's Personality: An Exploratory Essay," *French Historical Studies* (Spring, 1971) 7:7.

2. Nada Tomiche, *Napoléon ecrivain*, pp. 11–12.

3. Parker, pp. 11–16 *passim*.

4. Tomiche, p. 20.

5. Abbé Augier de Marigny (1762–?), whom Quérard calls mediocre, wrote two multivolume histories of the Arabs and a general history of the twelfth century. Napoleon read his *Histoire des Arabs sous le gouvernement des Califes*, which appeared in 1750.

6. Terray is too obscure to be listed in Quérard or the general catalogue of the Bibliothèque Nationale but Napoleon read his *Mémoires*.

7. François Baron de Tott (1733–93), of Hungarian origin, was a French diplomat who served in Constantinople and the Crimea. He penned memoirs on the Turks and Tartars that earned him somewhat of a reputation for charlatanism.

8. Norwood Young, *The Growth of Napoleon: A Study in Environment*, pp. 164–66.

9. "J'etudias [sic] moins l'histoire que je n'en fis la conquête; c'est à dire que je n'en voulus et je n'en retins que ce qui pouvait me donner une idée de plus, dédaignant l'inutile et m'emparant de certains résultats qui me plaisaient." Tomiche, p. 18.

10. "A Citoyen Jérôme Bonaparte," August 6, 1802, in Léon Lecestre, ed., *Lettres inédites de Napoléon Ier*, 1: [389].

11. Napoleon I, "Observations sur un projet d'établissement d'une école spéciale de littérature et d'histoire au Collège de France," April 19, 1807, *Correspondance de Napoléon Ier* (hereinafter cited as *Correspondance de Napoleon Ier*), 15: 109–10.

12. Ibid., pp. 107–8.

13. Ibid., p. 107.

14. Ibid., p. 110.

15. Joseph Pelet de la Lozère, *Opinions de Napéléon sur divers sujets de politique et d'administration recueilles par un membre de son conseil d'état, et récit de quelques événemens de l'époque*, p. 168.

16. "A.M. Barbier," July 17, 1808, *Correspondance de Napoléon Ier*, 17: 399.

17. "Note pour M. Barbier," February 26, 1808, ibid., 23: 255.

18. "Note pour le ministre de l'intérieur," February 6, 1805, ibid., 10: 139.

19. Antoine-Alexandre Barbier (1765–1825), successively *bibliothécaire* of the council of state and of Napoleon, was a savant bibilographer who published catalogues of the collections under his care, dictionaries, and some critical pieces.

20. "Au Général Savary, duc de Rovigo," October 1, 1810, *Correspondance de Napoléon Ier*, 21: 160.

21. "Au Général Savary, duc de Rovigo," February 21, 1811, ibid., p. 412.

22. "Note pour M. Barbier," March 19, 1811, ibid., p. 494.

23. "A.M. Barbier," December 19, 1811, ibid., 23: 95.

24. "Note pour M. Barbier," January 7, 1812, ibid., p. 162.

25. Claude Fr. Baron de Méneval (1778–1850), secretary to Joseph Bonaparte before becoming Napoleon's from 1802 to 1812. The Emperor made him a baron in 1810.

26. *Correspondance de Napoléon Ier*, 23: 398.

27. "A.M. Barbier," September 30, 1812, ibid., 24: 234.

28. Ibid., 28: 300.

29. "Note pour M. Cretet," April 12, 1808, ibid., 16: 489.

30. "Observations sur les rapports du ministre de l'intérieur relativement à l'encouragement des lettres," April 19, 1807, ibid., 15: 97.

31. "Note pour M. Cretet," April 12, 1808, ibid., 16: 489 and 491.

32. "Note," April 29, 1803, *Correspondance de Napoléon Ier*, 8: 300.

33. Jean Baptiste Nompère de Champagny (1756–1834) was Napoleon's ambassador to Vienna from 1801 to 1804, minister of the interior from 1804 to 1807, when he succeeded

Talleyrand as minister for foreign affairs. He retired in 1811, after a quarrel with the Emperor, but he joined him during the Hundred Days.

34. "Décret," March 12 and 14, 1806, ibid., 12: 188.
35. "Au Cardinal Fesch," February 13, 1806, ibid., p. 40.
36. Peter Stadler, *Geschichtschreibung und historische Denken in Frankreich 1789–1871*, p. 57.
37. May 16, 1806, *Correspondance de Napoléon Ier*, 12: 374.
38. "Au Prince Eugène," July 22, 1807, ibid., 15: 444.
39. "Décret," May 17, 1809, ibid., 19: 15.
40. "Circulaire aux Evêques," November 6, 1809 in Léon Lecestre, 1: 376.
41. "Discours de M. Fontanes, grand-maître de l'université," *Le Moniteur universel*, November 17, 1809, p. 1272.
42. "A Citoyen Chaptal," February 9, 1803 in Lecestre, *Lettres inédites de Napoléon Ier*, 1: 39.
43. "Décision," December 12, 1806, *Correspondance de Napoléon Ier*, 14: 69.
44. "A.M. Cretet," October 2, 1807, ibid., 16: 63. Agnes Sorel (1422–50) was mistress of Charles VII of France from 1444 to 1450, and was the first to hold that semiofficial position in the monarchy's history. Charles was captivated by her great beauty and lavished wealth upon her. Her sudden death after the birth of her fourth child was attributed to poison. Much myth grew up around her career and her influence upon her royal lover.
45. See above, pp. 8–10.
46. "Vous devez comprendre que je ne me sépare pas de mes prédecesseurs, et que, depuis Clovis jusqu'au Comité de salut public je me tiens solidaire de tout," Letter to King Louis as quoted by Stadler, p. 57.
47. "Le respect de l'histoire est inconnu à cet homme qui ne conçoit le monde que comme contemporain de lui." Ibid.
48. "Note pour M. Cretet," April 12, 1808, *Correspondance de Napoléon Ier*, 16: 489–90.
49. Quoted by John Charpentier, *Napoléon et les hommes de lettres de son temps*, p. 91.
50. Tomiche, pp. 237–38.
51. Marchand and Las Cases as quoted by Tomiche, ibid., pp. 238–39. Napoleon did not keep all of these promises.
52. These are found in *Correspondance de Napoléon Ier*, Vol. 32.
53. Tomiche, pp. 241–43.
54. Ibid., pp. 246–47.
55. J. Christopher Herold, ed., *The Mind of Napoleon*, p. 58–59.
56. Quotations in this paragraph on French kings are from ibid., pp. 59–60.
57. Ibid., p. 67.
58. Ibid., pp. 65–66.
59. Ibid.
60. Ibid., pp. 50–51.

CHAPTER II

1. Annie Winsor Allen, "Pierre-Louis Roederer (1754–1835) Sa Vie et son oeuvre," pp. 136–38.
2. "Les enfants des citoyens peu fortunés, ceux des habitants des campagnes restant sans aucune ou presque aucune source d'instruction. Deux générations de l'enfance sont à peu près menacées de ne savoir ni lire, ni écrire, ni les premiers éléments de calcul. C'est dire combien il est instant que le gouvernement prenne des mesures pour remédier à ce

mal." Councilor of State Fourcroy, May, 1810, quoted by Georges Pariset, *Le Consulat et l'Empire*, p. 319.

3. Ibid., pp. 318–22.

4. Michelle Paucton-Grasset, "La Pédagogie familiale de l'époque napoleonienne (1800–1815)," *Revue de l'Institut Napoléon* (July 1967), 104: 117–18.

5. Born in 1754, Roederer was appointed director general of public instruction on 21 Ventôse, year X. He was recognized as a specialist on economics and legislation. An active member of the Institut, he had been one of the conspirators of 18 Brumaire. After the *coup d'état* he continued to associate closely with Napoleon. He became a member of the Council of State where he served as president of the Interior Section from Christmas Day of 1799 until September 14, 1802. In this capacity he worked closely with Napoleon and often dined *en famille* with the first consul at the Tuileries, Malmaison, and Mortefontaine; afterward, he recorded his conversations with Napoleon. These are published as *Conversations notées par le Comte Roederer*, ed. by Maximilien Vox, in the collection "Le Roman de l'Histoire." As long as he was director general of public instruction, Roederer had to implement Chaptal's plan for education and attend to all the details not covered by it. After the Restoration Roederer published some historical works on medieval French history. He lived until 1835. Allen, pp. 138–39, 199–241 *passim*.

6. Arch. Nat. 29 AP 75, pp. 394–95.

7. Ibid., p. 443.

8. Ibid., p. 666.

9. Preceding paragraph based on Arch. Nat. 29 AP 75, pp. 389 and 646–59.

10. Allen, p. 225.

11. "Discours prononcé par M. Roederer, orateur du gouvernement, sur le projet de loi relatif à l'Instruction publique, séance du 11 floréal an 10," Arch. Nat. 29 AP 75, p. 682.

12. Allen, pp. 233–35.

13. *Correspondance de Napoléon Ier*, 9: 201.

14. Jacques Godechot, *Les Institutions de la France sous la République et l'Empire*, p. 637.

15. Louis Grimaud, *Histoire de la liberté d'enseignement en France depuis la chute de l'ancien régime jusqu'en nos jours*, pp. 87–89.

16. Joseph Pelet de la Lozère, *Opinions de Napoléon sur divers sujets de politique et d'administration, recueillies par un membre de son conseil d'état, et récit de quelques événemens de l'époque*, p. 175.

17. "Note sur les lycées," February 16, 1805, *Correspondance de Napoléon Ier*, 10: 147–48.

18. See: Arch. Nat. F^{17} 8115–8127 passim for numerous examples of deaths, retirements, and the hiring of *répétiteurs*.

19. Jean-Jacques Régis de Cambacérès (1753–1824), duke of Parma, became archchancellor of the empire in 1804. He always followed Napoleon's instructions while ruling France during the Emperor's absences.

20. Jean Etienne Marie Portalis (1745–1807), who was responsible for drawing up the Code Civil, was a councilor of state. In 1801 he was placed in charge of public worship.

21. "A.M. Cambacérès," October 7, 1804, *Correspondance de Napoléon Ier*, 10: 12.

22. "Exposé de la situation de l'Empire," March 5, 1806, ibid., 12: 151.

23. "Note sur l'établissement d'Ecouen," May 15, 1807, ibid., 15: 225–27.

24. "Au Comte Bigot de Préameneu," July 13, 1810, in Lecestre, *Lettres inédites de Napoléon Ier*, 1: 51.

25. "Note sur l'établissement d'Ecouen," May 15, 1807, *Correspondance de Napoléon Ier*, 15: 229.

26. "Il serait bon qu'une commission fût chargée de taxer les livres classiques, adoptées par les lycées, à tant le feuille," "A.M. Champagny," March 9, 1805, ibid., 10: 205.

27. Antoine Sérieys, *Chefs-d'oeuvre d'éloquence tirées des Oeuvres de Bossuet*,

Fléchier, Fontenelle et Thomas, Adoptées par le Gouvernement, pour la classe des Belles-lettres, dans les Lycées et Ecoles secondaires, p. 338.

28. "Décision," April 2, 1807, *Correspondance de Napoléon Ier*, 15: 8.

29. "Projet de loi sur l'instruction publique et discours par A. F. Fourcroy, orateur du gouvernement, présenté au *Corps législatif* le 30 germinal, an X," p. 9 in Arch. Nat. 29 AP 75, p. 681.

30. "Observations sur un projet d'établissement d'une école spéciale de littérature et d'histoire au Collège de France, April 19, 1807," *Correspondance de Napoléon Ier*, 15: 107–8.

31. Ibid., pp. 106–7.

32. Amédée Edmond-Blanc interprets Napoleon's Observations to mean that the emperor planned actually to have twenty to thirty chairs for historical sciences. *Napoléon Ier Ses Institutions Civiles et Administratives,* p. 230.

33. "Observations sur un projet d'établissement d'une école spéciale de littérature et d'histoire au Collège de France, April 19, 1807," *Correspondance de Napoléon Ier*, 15: 107–8.

34. François Aulard, *Napoléon Ier et le monopole universitaire,* p. 127.

35. "Procès-verbal de la Séance du 16 fevrier 1810," Arch. Nat. F^{17}* 1753, pp. 17–22.

36. Ibid., pp. 22–23. Teaching the concordance of ancient and modern place names fell into the province of the professor of geography.

37. "Procès-verbal de la Séance du Ier fevrier 1811," Arch. Nat. F^{17}* 1754, pp. 33–34.

38. "Procès-verbal de la Séance du 6 avril 1810," Arch. Nat. F^{17}* 1753, pp. 54–63.

39. "Note sur les lycées," February 16, 1805, *Correspondance de Napoléon Ier*, 10: 144–47.

40. "Décison," September 16, 1807, ibid., 16: 38.

41. *Biographies des Grands Hommes et des Personnages Remarquables qui ont veçu sous l'empire,* pp. 294–95. Fontanes easily switched over to Louis XVIII during the Restoration.

42. Aileen Wilson, *Fontanes,* pp. 238–39.

43. Ibid., p. 257.

44. Rémy Tessonneau, *Joseph Joubert, Educateur,* p. 276.

45. Jean-Pierre Bachasson, count of Montalivet (1766–1823), named councilor of state in 1805, director general of roads and bridges in 1806, and minister of the interior in 1809.

46. "Au Comte de Fontanes," February 7, 1810, *Correspondance de Napoléon Ier*, 20: 191–92.

47. Tessonneau, p. 280.

48. Wilson, p. 263.

49. Henri de Riancey, *Histoire d'instruction publique et de l'enseignement en france,* 3: 215.

50. Wilson, p. 265.

51. Henry Buisson, *Fouché duc d'Otrante,* pp. 40 and 150.

52. Fontanes was Elisa Bonaparte's lover, which may explain why Napoleon favored and tolerated him at all.

53. Esmenard as quoted by Henri Welschinger, *La Censure sous le Premier Empire,* p. 120.

54. M.A. Bardoux, *Guizot,* p. 17.

55. Douglas Johnson, *Guizot,* p. 3.

56. Aulard, p. 343 and Godechot, p. 652.

57. For example, see: "Bulletin of March 13, 1809," in Ernest d'Hauterive, ed., *La Police Secrète du Premier Empire,* 4: 572.

58. "Notes sur les *Lettres* de Hobhouse," 1816, *Correspondance de Napoléon Ier*, 31: 224.

59. H.A.L. Fisher, *Napoleon,* p. 92.

60. Aulard, p. 338.
61. Tessonneau, p. 274.
62. Godechot, p. 651.
63. "Au Comte de Montalivet, ministre de l'intérieur," November 30, 1811, *Correspondance de Napoléon Ier*, 23: 40.
64. Tessonneau, p. 275. Napoleon had made history part of the curriculum of *lycées*, however. See his Letter to Champagny, July 31, 1805. *Correspondance de Napoléon Ier*, 11: 50.
65. Summaries of these reports are contained in Charles Schmidt, *La Réforme de l'Université impériale en 1811*, pp. 59–119.
66. This term, *Quatrième Race*, was used during the Empire to refer to the Napoleonic Dynasty which superseded the first three French dynasties. The Merovingians were the *Première Race*, the Carolingians were the *Deuxième Race*, and the Bourbons were commonly called the *Troisième Race* by Imperial historians as well as by the emperor himself.
67. Arch. Nat. F^{17} 8119.
68. Some examples are Bouches-du Rhône, Charente, and Doire. Ibid., pp. 64, 66, and 72.
69. This was true in Aisne. Ibid., p. 61.
70. Finistère was one of these areas. Ibid., p. 75.
71. The *lycée* at Bourges in the department of Cher lacked these texts. Ibid., pp. 67–68.
72. Izarn, *Etat Actuel de l'Instruction publique*, pp. 58–59.

CHAPTER III

1. Antoine Sérieys, *Chefs-D'Oeuvre d'Eloquence tirées des Oeuvres de Bossuet, Flechier, Fontennelle et Thomas, Adoptés par le Gouvernement, pour la classe des Belles-lettres, dans les Lycées et Ecoles secondaire*, pp. 337–40.
2. "Bulletin du 12 janvier 1805," in Ernest d'Hauterive, ed., *La Police Secrète du Premier Empire*, 1: 244. See also: "Décision," February 4, 1811, *Correspondance de Napoléon Ier*, 21: 385–86.
3. Arch. Nat. F^{17} 8114.
4. Pamphlet cited, pp. 6, 8 and 14–15. Arch. Nat. F^{17*} 1752.
5. Summaries of these reports are contained in Charles Schmidt, *La Réforme de l'Université impériale en 1811*, pp. 59–119. See above, pp. 40–41.
6. "Procès-verbal de la Séance du 17 septembre 1811," Arch. Nat. F^{17*} 1754, p. 383.
7. At one session discussion began at two o'clock and lasted until five; alas, the minutes do not include any details about what was said during these three hours! "Procès-verbal de la Séance du 19 octobre 1813," Arch. Nat. F^{17*} 1756, p. 485.
8. "Procès-verbal de la Séance du 13 juillet 1813," ibid., pp. 342–49.
9. "Procès-verbal de la Séance du 29 octobre 1813," ibid., p. 488.
10. "Procès-verbal de la Séance du 7 decembre 1813," ibid., p. 535.
11. Napoleon took special interest in the continuations of older textbooks that he thought were "très-utile." See Napoleon's "Note pour M. Cretet," April 12, 1808, *Correspondance de Napoléon Ier*, 16: 489. Continuations of textbooks by Abbé Le Ragois were virtually new works.
12. "Sérieys," *Larousse Grand Dictionnaire universel du XIXe siècle*, 1874, 40: 595. See below, pp. 104–7.
13. "Le Prévost d'Iray," ibid., 10: 390.
14. "Chénier," *La Grande Encyclopédie*, 10: 1076.
15. "Domairon," *Biographie Universelle, Ancienne et Moderne*, 11: 499.
16. "Lacretelle le Jeune," *La Grande Encyclopédie*, 21: 722–23.
17. This idea sometimes presented a dilemma for historians who also believed that

modern history could not be understood without first teaching ancient history as a background. For example, see Pauline Meulan's review of *Bibliothèque des pères de Famille* in François Guizot, ed., *Annales d'Education*, 2: 101.

18. "Observations sur un projet d'établissement d'une école spéciale de littérature et d'histoire au Collège de France," April 19, 1807, *Correspondance de Napoléon Ier*, 15: 109.

19. Louis Domairon, *Rudiments d'histoire*, Vol. 3.

20. For example, Charles Mentelle, *Cours de Cosmographie, de Géographie, de Chronologie et d'Histoire ancienne et moderne, divisé en cent vingt-cinq Leçons*, 3: 407–23.

21. Antoine Sérieys, *Tablettes chronologiques à l'usage du Prytanée français* (1804). Of 333 pages, 71 are devoted to the papacy and 50 to China. About six editions, each continued to the year of publication, were published by 1816 and a seventh appeared posthumously in 1822.

22. Sérieys, *Tablettes chronologiques à l'usage du Prytanée avec des développemens historiques jusqu'à l'an 1805 inclusivement; Ouvrage adoptés pour la troisième classe des Lycées et Ecoles secondaires* (3rd ed., 1806), pp. 596–97.

23. Sérieys, *Eléments de l'histoire du Portugal contenant les causes de la grandeur et de la décadence des Portugais; leurs lois, leur commerce, les révolutions de ce royaume, etc.* Sérieys actually wrote only the preliminary discourse; the rest was written by Raynal and Madame de Sainctinge. See: Quérard, *La France Littéraire*, 9: 71.

24. Abbé C.-F.-X. Millot, *Eléments de l'histoire d'Allemagne*.

25. For example, Charles Mentelle told how Queen Elizabeth gave Virginia to Sir Walter Raleigh, and he praised George Washington, described the U.S. Constitution, and ended by quoting Pictet of Geneva, who, following Jedidiah Morse, had said that the very names of such cities as Philadelphia, Union, Concord, Salem, Hope—names of love, of fraternity, of peace, and of hope—beckoned to foreigners: "Ces noms parlent à Europe: ils semblent dire encore à nos peuples: Ne persécutez pas! ou vos citoyens passeront les mers." Charles Mentelle, *Cours d'Histoire; Seconde année . . .* pp. 150–66.

26. François Guizot, *Annales d'Education*, 1: 271.

27. Chrétien-Simeon Le Prévost d'Iray, *Tableau comparatif de l'histoire moderne ouvrage adoptée par le gouvernement etc.* (Imprimerie Impériale, 1804).

28. "Observations sur les rapports du ministre de l'intérieur relativement à l'encouragement des lettres," April 19, 1807, *Correspondance de Napoléon I*, 15: 97.

29. "Bon Dieu! que les hommes de lettres sont bêtes!" A M. Cambacérès," and "A M. Fouché," both dated January 24, 1806, ibid., 11: 554–55.

30. For example: Henri Engrand, *Leçons élémentaires sur l'histoire de France depuis le commencement de la Monarchie, jusqu'au 18 Brumaire an VIII, (de l'ère chrétienne 1800), à l'usage de la jeunesse de l'un et l'autre sexe* (2nd ed.; 1808). However, this textbook turns into a chronology at the beginning of the French Revolution.

31. Girard de Propiac, *Plutarque, ou abrégé des vies des Hommes illustres de ce célèbre écrivain avec des Leçons explicatives de leurs grandes actions; ouvrage élémentaire destinée à l'usage des Jeunes Personnes de l'un et l'autre sexe* (1804).

32. Propiac, *Le Plutarque des Jeunes Demoiselles, ou Abrégé des vies des Femmes illustres de tous les pays avec des leçons explicatives de leurs actions et de leurs ouvrages. Ouvrage élémentaire destiné à l'usage des jeunes personnes* (1806), 1: ii–vii.

33. Propiac, *Histoire de France de la Jeunesse* (1808).

34. Abbé Alouisine-Edouard-Camille Gaultier, *Leçons de Chronologie et d'Histoire* (1807). Various editions were reprinted several times, in full or part, between 1788 and 1823; it was finally continued to the reign of Charles X. The first part consisted of "Jeu de la chronologie & de l'histoire des rois de France," which had pictures of the kings and tokens for playing the game. Quérard, 3: 284.

35. This entire set was revised by Gaultier's pupils and reprinted in 1829. Quérard, 3: 285. François Guizot gave Gaultier flattering reviews in his journal *Annales d'Education*.

36. Gaultier, pp. vii-x. He says he gets his knowledge of the use of sensory perception in learning from M. de Buffon's article "Elephants," which he quotes. Napoleon also read Buffon when he was at Auxonne in March, 1789. N. Tomiche, *Napoléon Ecrivain*, p. 343.

37. These cards were on a fold-out sheet at the end of the first volume; lines were drawn on the sheet to indicate where to cut them apart. The example in the Bibliothèque Nationale was not colored, as stated in the preface. An English approximation of the poem on this flashcard is:

> The pontiff at Paris our ruler did crown,
> According to rules that God laid down.
>
> Thus did the pontiff the cross restore,
> Which Napoleon kneeling did adore.

38. Imperial authors defined "mutual instruction" as the study of two or more subjects simultaneously, not as older pupils teaching younger ones; the latter is the later nineteenth-century meaning.

39. Examples of nouns used in nominative case are Adam, Cain, Seth, etc., found on the pages indicated (p. 193). Adjectives of the genitive case are "Cult religieux," "Tête chauve," etc., found on the pages indicated (p. 194).

40. He did not believe in tolerating wild behavior and his 1812 treatise on the well-educated child set forth his rules of deportment: no making faces; do not sit with your mouth open or pull your tongue; do not come indoors smelling like the stable; no poking of other children; do not crack your knuckles or make hissing noises; no stamping of feet while walking around the classroom; no drumming of finger on furniture; do not put your pen, paper, or anything else in your mouth; do not take dirt off your hands with your saliva; do not look into your handkerchief after you blow into it; keep your fingers out of your nose; look at whoever is speaking to you and pay attention so repetition is not necessary; do not mumble, speak too softly, or use a monotonous tone of voice. *Traits caractéristiques d'une mauvaise éducation* (1812), pp. 2–6, 20, 25–26, 28, and 34.

41. Johann Heinrich Pestalozzi (1746–1827) was a radical, humanitarian Swiss educator who was influenced by Jean-Jacques Rousseau and who popularized and corrected his ideas. He envisioned a science of education based on the psychology of child development wherein teachers who were totally dedicated to their pupils guided them in discovering the real world around them and in developing their whole character. He also stressed mutual instruction with teacher and child learning with and from each other, something made possible by mutual bonds of love. His ideas became widespread through his moral novel *Léonard et Gertrude* (1781–87), *Comment Gertrude instruit ses enfants* (1801) and the *Livre des mères* (1803). In 1812, M.A. Jullien disseminated his ideas in *Esprit de la Méthode d'éducation de Pestalozzi*. Pestalozzi went to Paris and tried to interest Napoleon in a scheme of national education in 1802, but he received a cold response from the Emperor. Nevertheless, Pestalozzi is credited today with influencing the development of national school systems in the nineteenth century. He left thirteen volumes of writings.

42. Anne-François-J. Fréville, *Histoire des chiens célèbres, entremêlée de notices curieuses sur l'histoire naturelle pour donner le goût de la lecture à la jeunesse* (2nd ed.).

43. Michelle Paucton-Grasset, "La Pédagogie Familiale de l'époque Napoléonienne (1800–1815)," *Revue de l'Institut Napoléon* (July 1967), 104: 126.

44. The Academy of Sciences game is in Joachim Heinrich Campe, *Bibliothèque de l'enfance*, 2: 186–200.

45. See: "Au Comte de Montalivet, ministre de l'intérieur," October 11, 1814, *Correspondance de Napoléon Ier*, 24: 262.

46. Marie-François Desormes, *Histoire romaine, imitée d'Eutrope, et augmentée d'après Tacite, et autres historiens, à l'usage des Lycées et des écoles secondaires*, pp. 154–56.

47. Sérieys, *Elémens de l'Histoire des Gauls suivis de deux Vocabulaires, l'un Géogra-*

phique, et l'autre d'anciens Mots gaulois; d'une Table chronologique, et d'une Notice sur l'ancien état de Paris à l'usage de la Jeunesse (year XIII), pp. ix–xiii.

48. Sérieys, *Précis de l'abrégé chronologique de l'Histoire du Prés. Hénault adopté pour les lycées et les écoles secondaires* (1805), pp. 52–62 passim.

49. Hubert Wandelaincourt, *Cours d'Education pour les écoles du Premier Age* (1801), 2: 1. Sérieys and Pierre-Nicholas Chantreau also taught this idea in their numerous books.

50. Wandelaincourt, *Cours d'Education*, 2: 24.

51. Pierre Blanchard, *Le Plutarque de la Jeunesse* (2nd rev. ed.), 2: 35.

52. Edmonde Mentelle, *Cours d'Histoire; Seconde année* . . . , p. 69.

53. Sérieys, *Précis de l'abrégé chronologique de l'Histoire du Prés. Hénault adopté pour les lycées et les écoles secondaires*, pp. 153–63. This obviously was one of many attempts by Napoleon to profit from the people's love of Henry IV by drawing a parallel with the legendary king. See: Marcel Reinhard, *La Légende de Henri IV*, pp. 133–36.

54. Mentelle, *Cours de Cosmographie*. . . , 2: 191.

55. Pierre Blanchard, *Le Plutarque de la Jeunesse* (2nd rev. ed.), 3: 222.

56. Mentelle, *Cours d'Histoire; Seconde année* . . . , p. 85.

57. Sérieys, *Tables chronologiques de l'histoire ancienne et moderne avec des développemens historiques, jusqu'à la paix d'Amiens, à l'usage du Prytanée français* (year XI—1803), p. 415. In the fifth edition, published in 1817, these comments about Louis XIV (which also appeared in the 1807 edition) were omitted, whereas Sérieys kept the sections on Louis XV and Louis XVI exactly the same with the only addition being the death of Louis XVII and the "advent" of Louis XVIII on June 8, 1794. The 18 Brumaire was described exactly as in the 1803 ed. Work cited (5th rev. ed.; 1817), pp. 342–57 and 366.

58. Pierre Blanchard, *Beautés de l'Histoire de France* (2nd rev. ed.; 1810), pp. 436–37.

59. *Abrégé de l'Histoire de France à l'usage des élèves de l'école militaire* (1811), 2: 334.

60. Propriac, *Histoire de France de la Jeunesse* (1808), p. 603.

61. Engrand, *Leçons élémentaires sur l'histoire de France depuis le commencement de la Monarchie, jusqu'au 18 Brumaire an VIII, (de l'ère chrétienne 1800), à l'usage de la Jeunesse de l'un et l'autre sexe*, p. 216.

62. Blanchard, *Beautés de l'Histoire de France*, pp. 437–48 passim.

63. Propriac, *Abrégé de l'Histoire de France*, 2: 196.

64. Ibid., pp. 221–22.

65. Ibid., p. 223.

66. Ibid., p. 334.

67. Work cited (4th ed.; 1812), pp. 437–40.

68. Hauterive, 2: 417.

69. See: Sérieys, *Epitomé de l'Histoire de France . . . jusqu'au couronnement de Napoléon Ier., Empereur des Français; Ouvrage destiné à l'Enseignement des Lycées, des Ecoles secondaires, et des pensionats des deux sexes* (1805), p. 508.

70. Propriac, *Histoire de France de la Jeunesse*, pp. 585–86.

71. Ibid., pp. 586–87.

72. Ibid., pp. 608–13 passim.

73. Ibid., p. 620.

74. Pierre-Nicholas Chantreau, *Histoire de France* (1808), 2: 425–26.

75. Abbé Claude Le Ragois, *Instruction sur l'histoire de France et sur l'histoire romaine* (1810), p. 306.

76. *Epitomé de l'Histoire des Papes; Ouvrage élémentaire à l'usage des Jeunes Gens* (1805), pp. 207–8.

77. Sérieys, *Histoire Abrégée de la Campagne de Napoléon-le-grand en Allemagne et en Italie—jusqu'à la paix de Pressbourg* (1805).

78. Chantreau, *Histoire de France*, 1: 1.

79. Girard de Propriac, *Histoire de France de la Jeunesse*, p. 662.

80. Le Ragois, pp. 321–22. Prize-ceremonial speakers were brought in to reinforce what the children learned in their textbooks. For example, Samuel Bernard told the

children at the Collège de Rochefort that France was a monarchy [1810] because that was the only form of government suitable for such a vast empire. He went on to tell the youngsters that even if the government was imperfect they should respect it: "Nos annales n'offrent que trop d'exemples des suites funestes de l'esprit inquiet et séditieux; la Ligue, la Fronde, et sur-tout la Révolution sont des preuves mémorables des funestes effets de l'anarchie." He also defended the Napoleonic dynasty: "Vos maîtres et vos Magistrats mettront donc sous vos yeux et recommanderont à votre vénération, les images et les statues explits, à cherir ses bienfaits, à connaître les monumens par lesquels il éternise chaque jour le souvenir de son règne." *Discours prononcé par Mr. Samuel Bernard à la distribution solennelle des prix décernés aux élèves du collège de Rochefort le 15 septembre 1810.*

81. Le Prévost d'Iray, *Histoire Ancienne* (2nd ed.; Imprimerie Impériale, 1804).

82. See: "A l'Archevêque de Paris," August 28, 1802, and "Au Citoyen Portalis," December 18, 1802, *Correspondance de Napoléon Ier*, 8: 8 and 141. Sérieys wrote a three-volume work on the spread of Christianity in Siam, China, and Japan in the sixteenth, seventeenth, and eighteenth centuries at this time: *Histoire de l'Etablissement du Christianisme dans les Indes Orientales* (1803).

83. Sérieys, *Tables chronologiques de l'histoire ancienne et moderne avec des développemens historiques, jusqu'à la paix d'Amiens, à l'usage du Prytanée Français*, pp. 62–63 and Jean Picot, *Tablettes chronologiques de l'histoire universelle, sacré et profane, ecclésiastique et civile depuis la création du monde jusqu'à l'année 1808. Ouvrage Rédigé d'après celui de l'abbé Lenglet du Fresnoy*, . . . (1808), 1: 519–22.

84. Le Prévost d'Iray, *Histoire Ancienne* (2nd ed.).

85. *Récits des Temps Merovingiens, précédés de considerations sur l'Histoire de France*, 1: 11–13.

CHAPTER IV

1. "Décret," February 6, 1802, *Correspondance de Napoléon Ier*, 7: 378.

2. "A M. Cambacérès," December 15, 1806, ibid., 14: 89. In the organization of the government, the Department of the Chief Judge controlled the Imprimerie de la République, which was authorized to print laws, etc.; from 1804 to 1809 "on y imprime aussi quelques Ouvrages particuliers qui peuvent être intérressans pour les sciences et les arts, et lorsque leur publication est dans le cas d'être facilitée et encouragée." *Almanach national de France, an XII de la République*, p. 104.

3. "Au Général Berthier," April 5, 1804, ibid., 9: 318.

4. See: "Décision," March 27, 1805, ibid., 10: 265 and "Décision," February 4, 1811, ibid., 21: 385–86.

5. "Au Comte de Montalivet, ministre de l'intérieur," January 3, 1810, and "A M. Fouché," January 9, 1810, ibid., 20: 98 and 105.

6. For example, Napoleon hired Lemontey to write a history of France since the death of Louis XIV in order to show the decadence of the Bourbons. "A M. Lemontey," November 12, 1806, ibid., 13: 521.

7. "Décision," March 9, 1804, ibid., 9: 275.

8. "Au Prince Eugène," June 19, 1805, ibid., 10: 537.

9. See: Henri Welschinger, *La Censure sous le Premier Empire*, for a complete analysis of all aspects of Imperial censorship.

10. See: "A M. Fouché," June 1, 1805, *Correspondance de Napoléon Ier*, 10: 466 and "Au Prince Eugène," June 19, 1805, ibid., pp. 536–37.

11. "Décision," October 10, 1812, and "Au Comte de Montalivet, ministre de l'intérieur," ibid., 10: 261–62. In 1812 local inspectors seized books they thought were obscene or favored the Bourbon regime. These they forwarded to Baron de Pommereul, who was general director of the Imprimerie and Librairie, and he in turn forwarded them

to minister of interior Montalivet. For an example in which five history books were seized at Lille see: Arch. Nat. F[18] 11 B, Plaq. 4, pp. 19–20.

12. "Note pour M. Cretet," April 12, 1808, ibid., 16: 489.

13. *Journal Général*, 17: 144. On the other hand, Michaud claimed in 1815 that the publication of several entire volumes of Sismondi's *Histoire des républiques italiennes du moyen âge* was stopped. *Journal Général*, 18: 237.

14. For example see: "Bulletin du 3 novembre 1804," and "Bulletin du 10 novembre 1804," in Ernest d'Hauterive, ed., *La Police Secrète du Premier Empire*, 1: 158: and 168.

15. "A M. Fouché," February 2, 1807, *Correspondance de Napoléon Ier*, 14: 276.

16. "Au Général Savary, duc de Rovigo, ministre de la police générale," February 26, 1814, ibid., 27: 247.

17. For example, the editor of the *Publiciste* was fired by executive order for this. March 24, 1808, ibid., 16: 436.

18. "A M. Fouché," May 7, 1806, ibid., 12: 358.

19. "Bulletin du 25 octobre 1806," in Ernest d'Hauterive, ed., 3: 36. For two examples also see: "Bulletin du 29 decembre 1804," in Hauterive, 1: 227. The fifth edition of Antoine Ferrand's book on the study of history (see above, p. 79) could not be announced. *Journal Général*, 17: 144.

20. See: *Le Moniteur*, passim. Many of these reviews were written by Tourlet, Pechet, and Verneur. Naturally, the censors supervised these reviewers.

21. Ch. -V. L. "Institut de France," *La Grande Encyclopédie*, 20: 842.

22. Ibid., pp. 841–42.

23. *Histoire et Mémoires de l'Institut Royal de France, Classe d'Histoire de Littérature ancienne*, 1: 1. The following paragraph is from this source.

24. Napoleon's decree of 3 Pluviôse, year XI, organized the history class; a second decree of 8 Pluviôse, year XI, named the membership of the class. Both are printed in ibid., pp. 2–11.

25. *Organisation et Réglèmens de l'Institut National*, 3: 30–35.

26. Article I–VIII, ibid., pp. 84–88.

27. Article IX., ibid., p. 89.

28. Ibid., p. 90.

29. Ibid., pp. 92–95.

30. Ibid., p. 100.

31. Ibid., pp. 11–19. That a compromise was actually arranged is confirmed by the register of 9 Floréal, year XI, when the *secrétaire perpétuel* noted the reception of a letter from the minister of interior saying that the class's decisions of 10 and 17 Germinal were contrary to the law of 3 Pluviôse and, therefore, they would have to deliberate further. The first consul approved the final results of their deliberations on 26 Floréal. *Institut National des Sciences et Arts*, 3: 102.

32. "Décision," June 24, 1803, *Correspondance de Napoléon Ier*, 8: 374.

33. *Histoire et Mémoires de l'Institut Royal de France, Classe d'Histoire et de Littérature ancienne*, 1: 19. The members of the Institut even gave Napoleon a "patriotic gift," in August, 1803, of 6,000 francs to be deducted from their salaries to help defray the expenses of the war. See: Cambacérès, *Lettres inédites à Napoleon* (1802–1814), 1: 98.

34. *Institut de France*. 3e *Classe. Travaux divers* 1803–1816, ibid., 15: 1. The call number for this at the Bibliothèque Mazarine is AA 34, tome 15.

35. Ibid., 1: 20.

36. Ibid., p. 260.

37. Ibid., p. 21.

38. Ibid., pp. 260–64.

39. Ibid., pp. 22–23.

40. Letter cited, May 27, 1807, ibid., pp. 23–25.

41. Ibid., pp. 25–26.

42. "Décret," September 11, 1804, *Correspondance de Napoléon Ier*, 9: 2.
43. "Décret Impérial du 28 novembre 1809," *Le Moniteur universel*, December 3, 1809, 40: 1335–36, and Godechot, p. 653.
44. "Décision," August 31, 1808, *Correspondance de Napoléon Ier*, 17: 482 and "Au Prince Cambacérès, archichancelier de l'Empire," November 26, 1808, ibid., 28: 79.
45. "Décret Impérial du 28 novembre 1809," *Le Moniteur universel*, December 3, 1809, 40: 1335–36.
46. *Histoire et Mémoires de l'Institut Royal de France, Classe d'Histoire et de Littérature ancienne*, 1: 26.
47. "Note pour le ministre de l'intérieur," December 9, 1810, *Correspondance de Napoléon Ier*, 21: 311–12.
48. Jacques Godechot, *Les Institutions de la France sous la Révolution et l'Empire*, p. 653.
49. "Prix décennaux," *Le Moniteur universel*, July 17, 1810, 43: 782–83.
50. Ibid.
51. Ibid.
52. Amédée Edmond-Blanc, *Napoléon Ier, Ses Institutions Civiles et Administratives*, p. 234. See Quérard, *La France Littéraire*, 8: 282–83, for the details relating to the publication of this book.
53. *Histoire et Mémoires de l'Institut Royal de France, Classe d'Histoire et de Littérature ancienne*, 1: 27.
54. *Le Moniteur universel*, July 13, 1809, p. 763.
55. Ibid., p. 767.
56. Ibid., pp. 763–64.
57. Ibid., July 8, 1809, pp. 747–48.
58. Camille Louis Jullian, *Extraits des Historiens français de XIXe siècle*, p. IX.
59. *Le Moniteur universel*, December 27, 1809, 40: 1430.
60. Ibid., July 13, 1809, p. 768.
61. Godechot, p. 653.
62. *Histoire et Mémoires de l'Institut Royal de France, Classe d'Histoire et de Littérature ancienne*, 1: 28–29. The fact that questions 2 and 4 had no historical aspect went entirely unnoticed. The inference is that history, morality, and thought processes were conceived as interrelated and inseparable.
63. Ibid., p. 29. In 1818 he became a member of the Académie des Inscriptions.
64. Ibid.
65. Ibid., pp. 29–30.
66. Ibid., pp. 30–31. Figuring 1,500 and 1,000 francs for one subject and 1,500 for the other one, which was shared by two men.
67. *Ibid., p.* 31
68. Arch. Nat. F¹⁸ 11B, Plaq. 1, p. 3.
69. "Projet de Réglement général pour la Librairie et les professions en dépendantes," in ibid., Plaq. 4, Pièces Diverses 1812–13, p. 13.

CHAPTER V

1. This was the 1814 edition. According to Quérard this book may have gone through forty-eight editions. *La France Littéraire*, 5: 201–2.
2. Camille Louis Jullian, *Extraits des Historiens français du XIXe siècle*, p. VI, and "Lenoir," *La Grande Encyclopédie*, 22: 10.
3. For a full treatment of the importance of classical antiquity in the Revolution see: Harold T. Parker, *The Cult of Antiquity and the French Revolutionaries*.

70. *Notice Elémentaire sur l'origine, la Fondation et les Changemens qu'ont éprovés pendant leur durée les Empire et Etats dont il est fait mention dans l'Histoire Ancienne et Moderne de l'Europe, de l'Asie et de l'Afrique; pour servir à l'étude de la Mappemonde chronographique de l'ancien Continent* (1804), pp. v–viii.

71. Work cited, 1: i.

72. Ibid., p. ii.

73. Ibid., pp. ii–iii.

74. Ibid., p. vi.

75. See: Julian H. Franklin, *Jean Bodin and the Sixteenth Century Revolution in the Methodology of Law and History*; George Huppert, "The New History of the French Renaissance" and "The Renaissance Background of Historicism," *History and Theory*, 5: 48–60; Samuel C. Kinser, "The Historiography of J.A. de Thou."

76. Chantreau, *Science de l'Histoire*, 1: ix.

77. Pierre-Charles Lévesque (1736–1812), historian and translator, wrote several histories of France and Russia. L.P. Anquetil (1723–1808) was a member of the Institut de France who wrote histories of France and a multivolume world history. Jacques Hardion (1686–1766) was a man of letters who belonged to the Académie française. In addition to various dissertations on ancient literature he produced a twenty-volume universal history.

78. Chantreau, *Science de l'Histoire*, 1: xviii–xxv.

79. Ibid., pp. xv and xviii.

80. Ibid., pp. xv–xvi.

81. Ibid., p. xvii.

82. Ibid., p. 350.

83. Ibid., p. 485.

84. Ibid., 2: *avertissement*.

85. *Elémens d'histoire militaire* . . . (1808).

86. Ibid., pp. 2–3.

87. *Histoire de France* (1808).

88. Ibid., 1: x.

89. Ibid., p. xxiv.

90. Ibid., p. lxiv.

91. Ibid., p. lxxxvii.

92. Ibid., p. xcix.

93. Ibid., pp. cxxiii–clxxiv.

94. Ibid., pp. cci–ccii. Ameilhon lived until 1811, Lévesque until 1812, Kock until 1813, Servan until 1808, and Lacrettelle until 1855.

95. Ibid., p. ccclv.

96. Ibid., 2: 179, 182, 228, 476–77, 490 and 497.

97. Ibid., pp. 645–48.

98. Ibid., pp. 726–27. The last two verses of this are of particular interest:

> Héros de la France et de Rome
> Napoléon le Grand rassemble tous vos traits.
> Pour sauver un tel peuple il fallait un tel homme;
> Le ciel pour nous le fit exprès.
> Il le fallait guerrier, et pourtant pacifique.
> Du siècle ou triompha l'esprit philosophique
> Tout l'éclat devait l'entourner.
> Par sa haute valeur, par sa raison profonde,
> Il devait faire en tout l'étonnement du monde;
> Vaincre l'Europe et l'éclairer.
>
> Clio, recommence nos fastes;
> Un siècle tout nouveau s'ouvre pour les Français.

Napoléon les guide aux destins les plus vastes;
Lui seul peut borner ses succès.
C'est l'homme de l'Histoire et de la Providence.
Sa main ferme et rapide a de leur décadence
Relevé le trone et l'autel.
Grand Dieu! conserve-nous cette âme généreuse!
Que son nom soit béni! Que dans sa race heureuse
Son empire soit immortel!

99. Ibid., pp. 728–29.
100. "Lemontey," *La Grande Encyclopédie*, 21: 1200.
101. Henri Welschinger, *La Censure sous le Premier Empire*, pp. 20 and 67.
102. Cambacérès, 2: 777.
103. "A M. Lemontey," November 12, 1806, *Correspondance de Napoléon Ier*, 13: 521, and "Décision," February 4, 1811, ibid., 21: 385–86.
104. Quérard, 5: 151.
105. Jullian, p. X.
106. Letter of January 27, 1820. Arch. Nat. 20 AP 11. Lemontey had just read Roederer's *Histoire de Louis XII*, which he said was a fine example of the new history.

CHAPTER VI

1. "Note pour le ministre de l'intérieur," February 6, 1805, *Correspondance de Napoléon Ier*, 10: 139.
2. "Note pour le ministre des relations extérieures," February 14, 1810, and "Au Comte de Montalivet, ministre de l'intérieur," February 15, 1810, ibid., 20: 219–20.
3. *Tableau systématique des Archives de l'Empire.*
4. "Notice Générale des Ouvrages imprimés déposés à la Direction de l'Imprimerie et de la Librairie" and "Notice Générale par ordre de matières de tous les ouvrages imprimés déposés à la Direction de l'Imprimerie et de la Librairie," Arch. Nat. F¹⁸ 11B, plaq. 3 and plaq. 4, p. 26.
5. Stanley Mellon cited these numbers as pages. See: *The Political Uses of History*, p. 1.
6. These figures were estimated by counting the number of works on each topic listed in André Monglond's bibliography *La Fance révolutionnaire et impériale*.
7. Jullian, p. IX.
8. A.-H. Dampmartin, *La France sous ses rois; essai historique sur les causes qui ont préparé et consommé la chute des trois premières dynasties* (1810), 1: xxii.
9. Wandelcourt, *Cours d'éducation pour les écoles du second âge ou des adolescens* (1802), 3: 3–9.
10. M.-A. Moithey, *Abrégé de l'histoire de France depuis Clovis, jusques et y compris le règne de Louis XVI* (1810).
11. Kock, *Tableau des Révolutions de l'Europe depuis le Bouleversement de l'Empire romain en Occident, jusqu'à nos jours précédé d'une introduction sur l'histoire, et orné de cartes geographiques, de tables généalogues et chronologiques* (1807), 1: 1.
12. Charles-François Volney, *Leçons d'Histoire prononcés à l'école normale l'an III de la république française* (year VIII), p. 2.
13. For example, Bernardi, *Essai historique sur l'abbé Suger, Régent du Royaume, sous le Règne de Louis-le-jeune* (Paris: 1807) and Philippe Grouvelle, *Mémoires historiques sur les Templiers, ou Eclaircissements Nouveaux sur leur Histoire, leur Procès, les Accusations intentées contr'eux, et les Causes secrètes de leur Ruine; puisés, en grand partie dans plusieurs Monumens ou Ecrits publiés en Allemagne* (1805).

14. Gillot, *Dictionnaire des Constitutions* (1806).

15. Saint-Genois, *Monumens anciens* (1782–1804).

16. De-La-Varenne, *Histoire particulière des événemens qui ont eu lieu en France pendant les mois de juin, juillet, d'août et de septembre* 1792 (1806), pp. 419–520.

17. P.-A. Barbey-Duquil, *Le Tems ses Evénemens et Morts de marques* (1806).

18. Charles-François Volney, pp. 15–16.

19. *Annales de l'Empire Française* (1805), p. vii.

20. Ibid., p. viii.

21. Volney, pp. 16–17.

22. Ibid., pp. 65–69.

23. "Discours prononcé pour l'ouverture du Cours d'histoire moderne de M. Guizot, le 11 decembre 1812," in François Guizot, *Mémoires* 1: 390.

24. Court de Gébelin, "Du Scepticisme Raisonné de l'Histoire," in J.-L.-H.-S. Desperthes and J. François Née de la Rochelle, *Le Guide de l'Histoire à l'usage de la Jeunesse, et des personnes qui veulent la lire avec fruit ou l'écrire avec succès: Recueil Elémentaire* (1803), 1: 13.

25. Flassan, *Apologie de Histoire de la Diplomatie française* (1812), pp. 217–18.

26. Ibid., pp. 218–20.

27. Ibid., p. 225.

28. Satire published in Desperthes and Née de la Rochelle, I, 362–71 and reprinted from the *Conservateur*. This anthology was adopted by the government for the libraries of *lycées* in 1806. Work cited, p. 5.

29. Maurice Rivoire, *Précis Historique de la surprise d'Amiens par les espagnols le 11 mars* 1579 . . . *précédé d'un coup-d' oeil militaire sur le départment de la Somme* (1806).

30. See above, p. 51.

31. Koch, pp. V–VI.

32. Ibid., pp. VII–IX.

33. Volney, pp. 29–30.

34. Ibid., p. 32.

35. François Guizot, ed., *Annales de l'éducation* (1811), 2: 258.

36. Ibid., p. 265.

37. For example see his *Essai historique sur les Lois et Institutions qui ont gouverné la France sous ses premiers rois* (1811).

38. For example, see *Mélanges de Sacy. Mémoire sur une correspondance inédite entre Tamerlan et le roi de France Charles VI. Lu dans la séance de la Classe d'histoire et de littérature ancienne de l'Institut de France, du vendredi 3 juillet* 1812. Extrait du Moniteur, Nos 226 (an 1812*)*.

39. Gaillard, *Observations sur l'Histoire de France de Messieurs Velly, Villaret et Garnier* (1807).

40. Gaillard, *Histoire de la Rivalité de la France et de l'Espagne* (2nd. ed.; 1808), 8: 259–96. Gaillard's book was selected by the grand master of the Imperial University as a book prize for the *Concours* of 1813. Arch. Nat. AJ^{16} 881.

41. Barillet, *Recherches historiques sur le Temple* (1809), pp. viii–ix.

42. For example, Lenglet, *Révolutions du Globe* (1812). Lenglet also told how animal fossils found in rocks prove that water once covered the earth, and that coal and oil are products of animal life. Work cited, pp. 208–10.

43. Koch, *Tableau des Révolutions de l'Europe* (1807).

44. For example, see an anonymous work: *Histoire des Révolutions de France, depuis le commencement de la Monarchie jusqu'en* 1788, *avec des Réflexions sur leurs causes & leurs motifs, pour faire suite à celles de Vertot & d'Orléans, & c.* (1801), 1: 1.

45. Pierre Laboulinière, *Considérations politiques sur la France et les divers Etats de l'Europe* (1808), p. 28. However, he did not win the prize.

46. François Guizot, *Annales de l'éducation*, 2: 266.

47. V.D. Musset-Pathay, *Recherches historiques sur le cardinal de Retz; suivies des portraits, pensées et maximes extraits de ses Ouvrages* (1807), pp. 2–3.

48. Ibid., p. 3.

49. Portalis *fils, Du Devoir de l'Historien, de bien considérer le caractère et le génie de chaque siècle en jugeant les grands hommes qui y ont vécu; Discours couronné par l'Académie royale des Inscriptions et Belles-Lettres, Histoire et Antiquités de Stockholm, en mars 1800* (year VIII), pp. 7–8.

50. Ibid., pp. 11–12.

51. Louis Dubroca, *Les Quatre Fondateurs des Dynasties Françaises, ou histoire de l'établissement de la Monarchie française, par Clovis; du renouvellement des Dynasties royales, par Pépin et Hugh Capet, et de la fondation de l'Empire Français, par Napoléon-le-Grand* (1806), p. 252.

52. Moithey, 3: 222.

53. Guillaume, *Examen Critique d'une brochure intitulée Huges Capet* (1805), pp. 19–20. For other examples see P. Laboulinière, *Histoire politique et civile des trois premières dynasties françaises, dans laquelle on présente la série chronologique des Evénements militaires, politiques et civils, avec des remarques suivies sur l'Etat de la Législation, de l'Administration Publique, des Croyances, des Moeurs, des Institutions et Etablissements de tous genres, de l'Agriculture, du Commerce, de l'Industrie, des Lettres et des Beaux-Arts, dans chaque siècle* (1808), 3: 449; and Louis Marie de Sade, *Histoire de la Nation française, Première Race* (1805), p. 433.

54. Dampmartin, p. xxv.

55. Anonymous, *Histoire des Révolutions de France, depuis le commencement de la Monarchie jusqu'en 1788, avec des Réflexions sur leurs causes & leurs motifs, pour faire suite à celles de Vertot & d'Orléans, &c.*, 1: 1–2.

56. Dampmartin, pp. xxvii–xxviii.

57. Dubroca, *Les Quatre Fondateurs des Dynasties Françaises*, pp. 10–12.

58. Gaëtan de Raxis de Flassan *Histoire générale et raisonnée de la diplomatie française* (1809), 1: 58 and 65.

59. Charles-François Volney, pp. 116–19.

60. Marcel Reinhard, *La Légende de Henri IV*, pp. 133–35.

61. M.-A. Moithey, 1: v.

62. "Les Voyages d'Adolphe," *Annales de l'Education* (1813), 5: 249–52.

63. Lacretelle, *Histoire de France pendant le dix-huitème siécle* (4th ed.; 1819), 1: 2 and 105.

64. *Journal général de la littérature de France* (1808), 11: 305.

65. Lacretelle, *Histoire de France pendant le dix-huitième siècle*, 1: 122.

66. Welschinger, *La Censure sous le Premier Empire*, pp. 200–01.

67. J.-L.-H.S. Desperthes and J. François Née de la Rochelle, *Le Guide de l'Histoire à l'usage de la Jeunesse, et des personnes que veulent la lire avec fruit ou l'écrire avec succès: Recueil Elémentaire* (1803), 3: 309–10 and 324.

68. De-La-Varenne, *Histoire particulière des événemens qui ont eu lieu en France pendant les mois de juin, juillet, d'août et de septembre 1792* (1806), pp. iii–iv.

69. See: *Journal général de la littérature de France* (1801), 4: 9–10.

70. Costard, *Le Louvre, Louis XV et sa cour* (1807), p. v.

71. Ibid., pp. 36–37.

72. Flassan, *Histoire générale et raisonnée de la diplomatie française*, 6: 104–107.

73. P.C. Lecomte, *Mémorial ou Journal historique impartial et anecdotique de la Révolution de France, contenant une série exacte des faits principaux qui ont amené et prolongé cette révolution, depuis 1786, jusqu'à l'armistice signé dans les dernières jours de l'an VIII; dans lequel la chronologie a été scrupuleusement observée, et òu l'on voit quantité de rapprochemens curieux, d'anecdotes héroiques, nationales satyriques, la plupart inédites* (1801), 1: 244–45.

74. B. Barère de Vieuzac, *De la Conduite des Princes de la Maison de Bourbon dupuis 1789 jusqu'en 1805 (1805), pp.* 17–18. In 1808, P. Laboulinière wrote essentially the same thing in his *Histoire politique et civile des trois premières dynasties françaises* . . ., 3: 442–43.

75. Pierre Laboulinière, *Histoire politique et civile des trois premières dynasties françaises* . . . (1808), 3: 449.

76. V.D. Musset-Pathay, *Souvenirs historiques ou coup-d'oeil sur les monarchies de l'Europe et sur les causes de leur grandeur ou de leur décadence* (1810), p. 141.

77. Dampmartin, *La France sous ses rois, etc.* (1810), quoted in the *Journal général de la littérature de France* (1810), 13: 105.

78. F. Emmanuel Toulongeon, *Histoire de France depuis la Révolution de 1789, Ecrites d'après les mémoires et manuscrits contemporains, recueillis dans les dépôts civils et militaires* (year IX—1801), : ii–v.

79. Anonymous, *Histoire de France depuis le 21 janvier 1793, époque de la mort de Louis XVI jusqu'au jour du couronnement de Napoléon premier* (1806), pp. 10–12.

80. For another example see: *Les Quinze, ou l'Histoire de la Grande Armée* (1801), p. 16.

81. *La Fin du 18ᵉ Siècle ou anecdotes curieuses et intéressantes, tirées de manuscrits originaux, de pièces officielles, ou transmises par les auteurs mêmes des faits, ou par des témoins non suspects; pour servir de matériaux, et de pièces justificatives, à l'Histoire de la République française, etc.* (1805–06), pp. 1–3.

82. Lecomte, 1: 96–97.

83. Sérieys, *La Fin du 18ᵉ Siècle*, pp. 27–29.

84. Barère de Vieuzac, p. 65.

85. Ibid., p. 74.

86. Lecomte, 1: 244.

87. Capelle, *Aneries Révolutionnaires* (1801), p. 100.

88. Sérieys, *La Fin du 18ᵉ Siècle*, pp. 6–9.

89. J.L. Soulavie aîné, *Mémoires historiques et politiques du règne de Louis XVI, depuis son mariage jusqu'à sa mort; ouvrage composé sur des pièces authentiques fournies à l'auteur avant la révolution, par plusieurs ministres et hommes d'état; et sur les pièces justificatives recueillies, après la 10 Août, dans les cabinets de Louis XVI à Versailles, à Rambouillet et au château des Tuileries* (year X), quoted in *Journal général de la littérature de France*, 4: 328.

90. A.F. Bertrand de Moleville, *Histoire de la Révolution de France pendant les dernières années du Règne de Louis XVI* (1801), 1: 23.

91. Toulongeon, 1: 1.

92. Review of Viller's *Essai sur l'esprit et l'influence de la réformation de Luther, ouvrage qui a remporté le prix sur cette question proposée dans la séance publique du 25 germinal an X, par l'Institut national de France* (1804) in *Journal général de la littérature de France*, 7: 85.

93. Review of Malleville *fils' Discours sur l'influence de la réformation de Luther, ouvrage dont il a été fait mention honorable dans la dernière séance publique de l'Institut national* (1804), in *Journal général de la littérature de France*, 7: 147.

94. *Journal général de la littérature de France*, 6: 48.

95. Lecomte, 1: 2.

96. Dubroca, p. 247.

97. Flassan, 7: 149–50.

98. Ibid., 6: 465–66.

99. Capelle, p. 144.

100. *Tableau d'une Histoire de la Révolution Française* (1801).

101. Capelle, p. 92.

102. Ibid., p. 121.

103. Jean Charles Lacretelle, *Précis historique de la révolution française—Convention national* (2nd ed.; 1806), quoted in the *Journal général de la littérature de France*, 9: 15.

104. Dubroca, pp. 247–48.

105. Ibid., p. 249.

106. Ibid.

107. Capelle, p. 131.

108. Dubroca, p. 250.

109. Capelle, pp. 143–44.

110. Jean Charles Lacretelle, *Précis historique de la Révolution Française. Directoire Exécutif* (1806), 1: iv–vi.

111. Ibid., 2: 4–5.

112. Ibid., 2: 3.

113. D.-F. Donnant, *Abrégé de l'histoire des Empereurs qui ont régné en Europe, depuis Jules-Caesar, jusqu'à Napoléon le Grand* (3rd ed.; 1811), p. 492.

114. N. Vitron de Saint-Allais, *La Verité rendue sensible à la nation français sur les effets de la révolution et sur l'administration du premier consul Bonaparte* (1803), p. 7.

115. Dubroca, p. 286.

116. Ibid., p. 287.

117. Anonymous, *Histoire du Directoire Exécutif de la République française depuis son installation jusqu'au dix-huit brumaire inclusivement suivie de pièces justificatives* (1801), p. 420.

118. Anonymous, *Histoire de France depuis le 21 janvier 1793, époque de la mort de Louis XVI jusqu'au jour du Couronnement de Napoléon premier*, p. 362.

119. Lecomte, 2: 320.

120. Anonymous, *Histoire de France depuis le 21 janvier 1793*, p. 363.

121. Jean-Charles Jumel, *Eloge de Charlemagne, empereur d'occident, dédié à M. le général de division Hulin* (1810), pp. 12–13.

122. Barbet de Bertrand, *Les Trois Hommes illustres ou Dissertation sur les Institutions politiques de César-Auguste, de Charlemagne et de Napoléon Bonaparte* (1803), p. 280.

123. Dubroca, pp. 324–26. For another example claiming Napoleon's uniqueness see: N. Vitron de Saint-Allais, *La France Militaire* (1812), 1: 17.

124. Dubroca, pp. 327–29.

125. Dampmartin, pp. xix–xxii.

126. Dubroca, pp. 245–47.

BIBLIOGRAPHY

1. SERIES OF PAPERS IN THE ARCHIVES NATIONALES

AJ^{16} 881—1813—III

29 AP 10, 11 and 75

F^{17} 8114–8127

F^{17}* 1752–54 and 1756

F^{18} 11B, Plaqs, 3–4.

2. IMPERIAL HISTORY TEXTBOOKS

Blanchard, Pierre. *Beautés de l'Histoire de France.* 2nd rev. ed. Paris: Blanchard et Cie, 1810.

Ceresa de Bonvillaret, Alexandre. *Précis historique de la Législation français à l'usage des élèves de la faculté de droit de Turin.* Turin: Au Palais de l'Académie, 1811.

Chantreau, Pierre-Nicholas. *Elémens d'histoire militaire.* . . . Paris: Amblecostes, 1808.

———. *Histoire de France abrégée et chronologique, depuis la première expédition des Gaulois jusqu'en septembre 1808,* 2 vols. Paris: Bernard, 1808.

———. *De l'importance de l'étude de l'histoire et de la vraie manière de l'enseigner, après un nouveau plan présenté par tableaux, qui contiennent les notions qu'il faut acquérir avant de se livrer à cette étude, et la méthode à suivre lorsqu'on s'y livre.* Paris: Deterville, year X.

———. *Notice Elementaire sur l'origine, la Fondation et les Changemens qu'ont éprouvés pendant leur durée les Empire et Etats dont il est fait mention dans l'Histoire Ancienne et Moderne de l'Europe, de l'Asie et de l'Afrique; pour servir à l'étude de la Mappemonde chronographique de l'ancien Continent.* Paris: by the author, 1804

———. *Mappemonde chronographique pour l'histoire ancienne et moderne . . . avec une explication qui en facilite l'usage.* Paris: 3, rue Christine, year XII—1803.

———. *Science de l'Histoire contenant le système général des connoissances à acquérir avant d'étudier l'histoire, et la méthode à suivre quand on se livre à ce gendre d'étude, developpée par tableaux synoptiques . . . Dediée au Premier Consul de la République Française,* 3 vols. Paris: Goujon fils, 1803–06.

————. *Tablettes chronologiques de l'histoire de France.* Fontainebleau: l'auteur, 1806.

Deperthes, Jean-Louis-Hubert-Simon. *Le guide de l'histoire, à l'usage de la Jeunesse et des personnes qui veulent la lire avec fruit ou l'écrire avec succès: Recueil Elémentaire,* 3 vols. Paris: Bidault, 1803.

Desormes, Marie François. *Histoire romaine, imitée d'Eutrope, et augmentée d'après Tacite, et autres historiens, à l'usage des Lycées et des écoles secondaires.* Paris: Guyon, 1807.

Domairon, Louis, *Rudiments d'histoire.* 3 vols. Paris: 1804.

Du Coeurjoly, S.-J. *Instruction de la Jeunesse ou notions élémentaires sur la Langue Français, la géographie, la mythologie, l'Histoire Grecque et Romaine, et l'Histoire de France,* 2 vols. Paris: Barba, 1805.

Engrand, Henri. *Leçons élémentaires sur l'histoire de France, depuis le commencement de la Monarchie, jusqu'au 18 Brumaire an VIII, (de l'ère chrétienne 1800). A l'usage de la Jeunesse de l'un et l'autre sexe.* 2nd ed. Reims: chez Le Batard, 1808.

Fantin-Des-Odards, Ant. -Et. -Nic. *Abrégé chronologique de l'Histoire de la révolution de France, à l'usage des écoles publiques,* 3 vols. Paris: Barba, 1802.

————. *Abrégé (nouv.) chronologique de l'Histoire de France, depuis la mort de Louis XIV, jusqu'au retour de Louis XVIII (formant la suite de l'ouvrage du président Hénault).* 3rd ed. Paris: 1807.

Gaultier, Abbé Alouisine-Edouard-Camille. *Leçons de Chronologie et d'Histoire,* 3 vols. Paris: chez l'auteur, 1807.

Girard de Propiac, Catherine-Joseph-Ferdinand. *Abrégé de l'Histoire de France à l'usage des élèves de l'école militaire.* Paris: 1811.

————. *Histoire de France de la Jeunesse, depuis l'établissement de la monarchie jusqu'au Ier janvier 1808; Ouvrage élémentaire destiné à l'usage des jeunes personnes de l'un et de l'autre sexe.* Paris: Gérard, 1808.

————. *Le Plutarque des Jeunes Demoiselles, ou Abrégé des vies des Femmes illustres de tous les pays avec des leçons explicatives de leurs actions et de leurs ouvrages. Ouvrage élémentaire destiné à l'usage des jeunes personnes,* 2 vols. Paris: Gérard, 1806.

————. *Plutarque, ou abrégé des vies des Hommes illustres de ce célèbre écrivain avec des Leçons explicatives de leurs grandes actions; ouvrage élémentaire destinée à l'usage des jeunes personnes de l'un et de l'autre sexe,* 2 vols. Paris: Gérard, 1804.

Goffaux, F. *Epoques principales de l'Histoire pour servir de précis explicatif au Tableau Chronométrique, indiquant l'origine, les progrès, la durée et la chute des Empires.* Paris: Dentu, 1805.

Koch, Christophe-Guillaume. *Tableau des Révolutions de l'Europe depuis le Bouleversement de l'Empire romain en Occident, jusqu'à nos jours précédé d'une introduction sur l'histoire, et orné de cartes géographiques, de tables généalogiques et chronologiques*, 4 vols. Paris: F. Schoell, 1807.

Lacretelle, Jean-Chârles le jeune. *Leçons élémentaires de l'histoire de France, depuis Pharamond jusqu'à l'année 1807, à l'usage des enfants des deux sexes.* Paris: Ponthieu, 1807.

———. *Nouvelles leçons élémentaires de l'histoire de France.* Paris: Ponthieu, 1806.

Le Prévost d'Iray, Vte Chrétien-Siméon. *Histoire Ancienne.* 2nd ed. Paris: Imprimerie impériale, 1804.

———. *Tableau comparatif de l'histoire ancienne, ouvrage élémentaire à l'usage des écoles publiques.* Paris: Imprimerie de la République, year X.

———. *Tableau comparatif de l'histoire moderne ouvrage adoptée par le gouv.* etc. XIII–1804. Paris: Imprimerie impériale, 1804 and 1807.

Le Ragois, Abbé Claude. *Instruction sur l'Histoire de France et sur l'histoire romaine, suivie d'un Abrégé des Metamorphoses d'Ovide, et d'un Recueil de Proverbes ou Sentences. Nouvelle Edition, corrigée et augmentée, contenant les événements les plus remarquables, jusqu'à l'heureux retour de Louis XVIII*, 2 vols. Avignon: Laurent Aubanel, 1810.

———. *Instruction sur l'histoire de France, par demandes et par réponses.* Paris: Augustin Delalain, 1810.

Mentelle, Edmonde. *Cours de Cosmographie, de Géographie, de Chronologie et d'Histoire ancienne et moderne, divisé en cent vingt-cinq Leçons*, 3 vols. Paris: Bernard, 1800–01.

———. *Cours d'Histoire; Seconde année. . . .* Paris: Mentelle, year X.

———. *Précis de l'Histoire universelle, pendant les dix premiers siécles de l'ère vulgaire, ou Introduction à l'Histoire moderne des différens Etats de l'Europe.* Paris: chez l'auteur, 1801.

Millot, Abbé. C.-F.-X. *Elémens de l'histoire d'Allemagne*, 3 vols. Paris: Le Normant, 1807.

Mir. *Cours élémentaire d'histoire. Epoques de l'histoire ancienne, à l'usage des jeunes personnes de l'un et de l'autre sexe*, 2 vols. Toulouse: By the author, 1803.

———. *Cours élémentaire d'histoire. Les cinquante-huit siècles bientôt écoles depuis la création de l'univers . . . précédés de notions préliminaires sur l'histoire et ses différentes divisions, à l'usage des jeunes personnes de l'un et l'autre sexe.* Toulouse: By the author, 1803.

Née de la Rochelle, Jean-François. *Le Guide de l'histoire à l'usage de la jeunesse.* Paris: Bidault, 1803.

Picot, Jean. *Tablettes chronologiques de l'histoire universelle, sacrée et profane, ecclésiastique et civile, depuis la création du monde jusqu'à l'année* 1808, 3 vols. Geneva: Manget et Cherbuliez, 1808.

Pornin, Antoine-François. *Abrégé de l'Histoire des Egyptiens, des Assyriens, des Babyloniens, des Mèdes, des Perses et des Scythes d'après les meilleurs auteurs et particulièrement Rollin et Bossuet à l'usage des maisons d'éducation.* Paris: Lebel et Guitel, 1810.

Pradel, P.-A. *Livre pour l'instruction de la jeunesse dans lequel on y trouve un Abrégé de l'histoire romaine, de l'histoire de France et un Abrégé de la géographie etc.* Paris: de Perreault, 1804.

Rougeron, P.N. *L'Historien des Jeunes Demoiselles.* Paris: Ancelle, 1810.

Sérieys, Antoine. *Elémens de l'Histoire des Gauls suivis de deux Vocabulaires, l'un Géographique, et l'autre d'anciens Mots gaulois; d'une Table chronologique, et d'un Notice sur l'ancien état de Paris. à l'usage de la Jeunesse.* Paris: Brasseur aîné, year XIII.

———. *Eléments de l'histoire du Portugal . . . Ouvrage qui peut servir à l'enseignement dans les Lycées, les Ecoles secondaires, et dans les Pensionats des deux sexes.* Paris: Demoraine, 1805.

———. *Epitome de l'histoire ancienne, contenant un précis de ses principales époques, suivie de l'Epitome de l'Histoire romaine de Sextus Rufus, traduit de Latin pour la première fois, avec des notes; Ouvrage Elémentaire.* Paris: Alexis Eymery, 1812.

———. *Epitome de l'Histoire de France contenant l'origine des Francs, leurs moeurs, leurs institutions, leurs lois, leur commerce, leurs progrès, dans les sciences et beaucoup d'anecdotes propres à les caracteriser, depuis l'Etablissement de la Monarchie jusqu'au couronnement de Napoléon Ier, Empereur des Français; Ouvrage destiné à l'Enseignement des Lycées, des Ecoles secondaires, et des pensionnats des deux sexes.* Paris: Samson, 1805.

———. *Epitome de l'Histoire des Papes; Ouvrage élémentaire à l'usage des Jeunes Gens.* Paris: Demoraine, 1805.

———. *Epitome de l'Histoire moderne, contenant les synchronismes des principales époques, depuis la chute de l'empire d'Occident jusqu'à* 1812. Paris: Eymery, 1812.

———. *Précis de l'Abrégé chronologique de l'Histoire de France, du président Hénault, adopté pour les lycées et les écoles secondaires; augmenté de plusieurs pièces inédites du même auteur, relatives à cette histoire; d'un choix de beaux traits historiques, recueillis par Millot, et continué jusqu'au sacre de Napoléon.* Paris: Demoraine, 1805.

———. *Tablettes chronologiques à l'usage du Prytanée, avec des développements historiques jusqu'à l'an* 1805 . . . *adopté pour la troisième classe des lycées* . . . 3rd ed. Paris: Obré, 1806.

————. *Tables chronologiques de l'histoire ancienne et moderne . . . jusqu'à la paix d'Amiens, à l'usage du Prytanée français.* Paris: Obré, 1803.

————. *Tables chronologiques de l'histoire ancienne et moderne, jusqu'à la paix d'Amiens, à l'usage du Prytanée français, contenant la fin de l'histoire moderne, et notamment celle des Pages et des Chinois, et formant la seconde et dernière partie des Tables chronologiques adoptées . . . pour l'enseignement des Lycées, . . .* Paris: Obré, 1804.

————. *Tablettes chronologiques de l'histoire ancienne et moderne, avec des développemens historiques, depuis la création du monde jusqu'à ce jour; Ouvrage anciennement adopté pour la 3ᵉ classe des Lycées et Ecoles secondaires.* 5th rev. ed. Paris: Eymery, 1817.

Tableau Chronologique, Généalogique et Historique de France Nᵒ 1 & 2. Paris: Didot l'Aîné, 1810.

Tableau Chronologique, Généalogique et Historique de la Maison d'Austriche. Nᵒ 1. Paris: Didot l'Aîné, 1810.

Tressan, Abbé Maurice-Elizabeth de Lavergnede. *La Mythologie comparée avec l'histoire, ouvrage destiné à l'éducation de la jeunesse,* 2 vols. Paris: J. Dufour, 1803.

Vertot et Saint Réal. *Les Révolutions de Portugal et la Conjuration des Espagnols contre Venise adoptées par le gouvernement pour la deuxième classe des lycées et écoles secondaires.* Paris: Demoraine, 1805.

Volney, Charles-François. *Leçons d'Histoire prononcés à l'école normale en l'an III de la république française.* Paris: J.A. Brosson, year VIII.

Le Voltaire de la Jeunesse. . . . Breslau: chez Guillaume Théophile Korn, 1809.

Le Voltaire de la Jeunesse ou choix de morceaux les plus propres à former le coeur et à orner l'esprit. . . . Paris: Chaumerot, 1808.

3. IMPERIAL HISTORY BOOKS

Audouin, Xavier. *Histoire de l'Administration de la Guerre,* 4 vols. Paris: P. Didot l'Aîné, 1811.

Badine, C.-F. *L'Ombre de Charles Fox au parlement d'Angleterre.* Paris: Dabin, 1808.

Barailon, J.F. *Recherches sur les peuples Cambiovicenses de la carte Théodosienne. . . .* Paris: Dentu, 1806.

Barbet du Bertrand, V.-R. *Les Trois Hommes illustres ou Dissertations sur les Institutions politiques de César-Auguste, de Charlemagne et de Napoléon Bonaparte.* Paris: Michelet, 1803.

Barbey-Duquil, Pierre-Augustin. *Les Tems ses Evénemens et Morts de marques, depuis 1 Année 1784, jusqu'en l'Année 1805.* Neufchâtel, Féray, 1805.

Barère de Vieuzac, B. *De la Conduite des Princes de la Maison de Bourbon depuis 1789 jusqu'en 1805.* Paris 1805.

Barillet, E.J.J. *Recherches historiques sur le Temple*. Paris: Dufour, 1809.

Barruel-Beauvert. *Actes des Philosophes et des Républicains*. Paris 1807.

Bayard de la Vingtrie, Ferdinand. *Tableau analytique de la Diplomatie française depuis la minorité de Louis XIII*. Paris: Prault, year XIII.

Beauchamp, Alphonse. *Histoire de la Guerre de la Vendée et des chouans depuis son origine jusqu'à la pacification de* 1800, 3 vols. Paris: Giguet et Michaud, 1806.

Beaunoir, Alexander-Louis-Bertrand Robineau and Dampmartin, A. H. *Annales de l'Empire Français*. Paris: Treuttel et Würtz, 1805.

Bernardi, Joseph-Elzéar-Dominique de. *Essai historique sur l'abbé Suger, Régent du Royaume, sous le Règne de Louis-le-jeune*. Paris: Impr. de Xhrouet, 1807.

——. *Essai sur la vie, les écrits et les lois de Michel de l'Hopital, Chancelier de France*. Paris: Petit, 1807.

Bertrand de Moleville, A. F. *Histoire de la Révolution de France pendant les dernières années du Règne de Louis XVI*, 14 vols. Paris: chez Giguet et Cie, 1801–03.

Blanchard, Pierre-Louis. *L'Etat politique et religieux de la France devenu plus déplorable encore par l'effet du Voyage de Pie VII en ce pays*. London: Cox, Fils, et Baylis, 1806.

——. *Histoire civile, politique et religieuse de Pie VI*. Avignon: n.d.

——. *Le Véritable Esprit du Catéchisme, à l'usage de toutes les Eglises de l'Empire français, qui vient d'être publié par M. Bonaparté. Instruction familière par Demandes et par Réponses adressée aux Fidèles de France*. London: Cox, Fils, and Baylis, 1806.

Boileau, Marie-Louis-Joseph de. *Entretiens critiques, philosophiques et historiques sur les procès*. Paris: Crapart, Caille et Ravier, year XII.

Braeckenier, A.J.D. *Journal Historique contenant les Evénemens et Faits les plus mémorables, tant Historiques, Diplomatiques que Politiques, avenue depuis le premier Octobre 1806 . . . rédigés Chronologiquement, et enrichis de Notes Géographiques, etc., etc.* Brussels: de Braeckenier, 1807.

Brayer de Beauregard, J.-B.-L. *L'Honneur français ou Tableau des Personnages qui, depuis 1789 jusqu'à ce jour, ont contribué, à quelque titre que ce soit, à honorer le nom français*, 2 vols. Paris: Leopold Collin, 1808.

Bülow, Heinrich Dietrich von. *Histoire de la Campagne de 1800 en Allemagne et en Italie par M. de Bülow, Officier Prussien, Auteur . . . de l'Allemagne et précédé d'une Introduction Critique, par Ch. L. Sevelingis*. Paris: Magimel, 1806.

Chahan de Cirbied, J.M. and Martin, F. *Recherches curieuses sur l'histoire ancienne de l'Asie*. Paris: Le Prieur, 1806.

Chaussard, Pierre-J.-B. *Jeanne d'Arc recueil historique et complet.* Orléans: Darnault-Maurant, 1806.

Choiseul-Daillecourt, Maxime. *De L'Influence des Croisades sur l'Etat des Peuples de l'Europe. Ouvrage qui a partagé le prix décerné par l'Institut, dans la Séance publique du 1er juillet 1808.* Paris: chez Tillard, 1809.

Costard, Jean-Pierre. *Le Louvre, Louis XV et sa Cour.* Paris: Frechet, 1807.

Dampmartin, Anne-Henri. *La France sous ses Rois; essai historique sur les causes qui ont préparé et consommé la chute des trois premières dynasties,* 5 vols. Paris: Le Normant; 1810.

Depiéreux, Madame C. *Les Beautés de l'histoire ou Tableau des vertus et des vices.* Paris: Jusserand, 1803.

Devismes du Valgay, A.-P.-J. *Nouvelles Recherches sur l'origine et la Destination des Pyramides d'Egypte. Ouvrage dans lequel on s'applique à demontrer que ces Merveilles renferment les principes élémentaires des Sciences abstraites et occultes, ainsi que ceux des Arts utiles à la Société: suivi d'une dissertation sur la fin du globe terrestre.* Paris: Charles, 1812.

Donnant, D.-F. *Abrégé de l'histoire des Empereurs qui ont régné en Europe, depuis Jules-César, jusqu'à Napoléon le Grand.* 3rd ed. Paris: Ferra aîné, 1811.

Dubroca, Louis. *Les Femmes Célèbres de la Révolution.* Paris: the author and Bonneville, 1802.

———. *Les Quatres Fondateurs des Dynasties Françaises, ou histoire de l'établissement de la Monarchie française, par Clovis; du renouvellement des Dynasties royales, par Pépin et Hugh Capet; et de la fondation de l'Empire Française, par Napoléon-le-Grand.* Paris: Dubroca, 1806.

Dumesnil, Alexis. *Le Règne de Louis XI et l'influence qu'il a eue jusque sur les derniers temps de la troisième dynastie.* Paris: Maradan, 1811.

Dumont de Florgy. *Histoire de Bohème depuis son origine jusqu'à l'extinction de la dynastie de Przémisel.* Vienna: Antoine Strauss, 1808.

Duverne de Praile, Th. *De la Guerre perpétuelle et de ses Résultats probables pour l'Angleterre.* Paris: Petit, n.d.

Fiévée, Joseph. *Des Opinions et des intérêts pendant la révolution.* Paris: Le Normant, 1809.

———. *Observations et projet de décret.* Paris: Imprimerie impériale, 1809.

Flassan, Gaëtan de Raxis de. *Apologie de Histoire de la Diplomatie français.* Paris: Debray, 1812.

———. *Histoire Générale et raisonnée de la diplomatie française,* 6 vols. Paris: Le Normant, 1809.

Gacon-Dufour, Madame. *La Cour de Catherine de Médicis, de Charles IX, de Henri III et de Henri IV,* 2 vols. Paris: Collin, 1807.

Gaillard, Gabr, -Henri. *Histoire de la Rivalité de la France et l'Espagne, contenant l'Histoire de la Rivalité, 1º des Maisons de France et d'Arragon, 2º des Maisons de France et d'Autriche; précedé d'un abrégé de l'Histoire ancienne de l'Espagne, servant d'Introduction*, 8 vols. 2nd ed. Paris: H. Nicolle, 1808.

⸻. *Observations sur l'Histoire de France de Messieurs Velly, Villaret et Garnier*, 4 vols. Paris: chez Xhrouet, 1807.

Gallet, Pierre. *Politique d'Auguste et de Charlemagne*. Versailles: Lebel et Guitel, 1810.

Gillot, C.-L. *Dictionnaire des Constitutions de l'Empire français et du royaume d'Italie*, 2 vols. Paris: J. Gratiot, 1806.

Girard de Villesaison. *Considérations sur les différens événemens qui ont contribué aux progrès de la civilisation en Europe depuis le XIIᵉ siècle jusqu'au XIXᵉ*. Paris: Theophile Barrois, 1810.

Grave, Charles-Joseph de. *République des Champs Elysées, ou Monde Ancien*, 3 vols. Grand: P.-F. de Goesin-Verhaeghe, 1806.

Grouvelle, Philippe-A. *Mémoires historiques sur les Templiers, ou Eclaircissemens Nouveaux sur leur Histoire, leur Procès, les Accusations intentées contr'eux, et les Causes secrètes de leur Ruine; puisés, en grande partie, dans plusieurs Monumens ou Ecrits publiés en Allemagne*. Paris: Buisson, 1805.

Guerin, Joseph-Xavier-Bénézet. *Discours sur l'histoire d'Avignon, suivi d'un apperçu sur l'état ancien et moderne de cette ville, et sur les monumens et les objets qui peuvent fixer l'attention des voyageurs*. Avignon: Guichard, 1807.

Guillaume, J.-L. *Examen critique d'une brochure intitulée Huges Capet*. Paris: 1805.

Hetzrodt, J. B. M. *Essai historique sur les Lois et Institutions qui ont gouverné la France sous ses premiers rois*. Treves: Hetzrodt, 1811.

Histoire de France depuis le 21 janvier 1793, époque de la mort de Louis XVI jusqu'au jour du Couronnement de Napoléon premier. Paris: Artaud, 1806.

Histoire des Révolutions de France depuis le commencement de la Monarchie jusqu'en 1788, avec des Reflexions sur leurs causes & leurs motifs, pour faire suite à celles de Vertot & d'Orléans, &c. Paris: La Vilette & Compagnie, 1801.

Histoire du Directoire Exécutif de la République française depuis son installation jusqu'au dix-huit brumaire inclusivement suivie de pièces justificatives. Paris: F. Buisson, 1801.

Histoire véritable de Fanchon la vieulleuse, extraite de Mémoires inédits, et ornée d'un portrait. Paris: Capelle, 1803.

Hüe, François. *Dernières Années du Règne et de la vie de Louis XVI*. Paris: l'imprimerie royale, 1814.

Jondot, E. *Tableau historiques des Nations ou rapprochement des principaux événemens arrivés, à la même époque, sur la surface de la terre; avec un aperçu général des progrès des Arts, des Sciences et des Lettres, depuis l'origine du monde jusqu'à nos jours,* 4 vols. Paris: Maradan, 1808.

Jullien du Ruet, D.-M. *Tableau chronologiques et moral de l'histoire universelle du commerce des anciens.* Paris: Garnery, 1809.

Jumel, Jean-Charles. *Eloge de Charlemagne, empereur d'occident, dédié à M. le général de division Hulin.* . . . Paris: Petit, 1810.

Koch, Christophe-Guillaume. *Tableau des Révolutions de l'Europe depuis le Bouleversement de l'Empire romain en Occident, jusqu'à nos jours précédé d'une introduction sur l'histoire, et orné de cartes géographiques, de tables généalogiques et chronologiques,* 4 vols. Paris: F. Schoell, 1807.

Laboissière, J. L. de. *Les Commentaires de Soldat du Vivarais, où se voit l'origine de la Rébellion de la France et toutes les guerres que, durant icelle, le pays du Vivarais a souffertes, divisés en trois livres, selon le temps que lesdites guerres sont arrivées; suivis du Voyage du Duc de Rohan de Roure, en 1670; De la Relation de la Révolte de Roure, en 1670; Et d'une Anecdote extraite du journal manuscrit de J. de Banne, Chanoine de Viviers.* Privas: F. Agard, 1811.

Laboulinière, P. *Considérations politiques sur la France et les divers Etats de l'Europe.* Paris: Dentu, 1808.

———. *De Influence d'une Grande Révolution sur le Commerce, l'agriculture et les arts.* Paris: Léopold Collin, 1808.

———. *Histoire politique et civile des trois premières dynasties françaises, dans laquelle on présente la série chronologique des Evénements militaires, Politiques et Civiles, avec des remarques suivies sur l'Etat de la Législation, de l'Administration Publique, des Croyances, des Moeurs, des Institutions et Etablissements de tous genres de l'Agriculture, du Commerce, de l'Industrie, des Lettres et des Beaux-Arts, dans chaque siècle,* 3 vols. Paris: Léopold Collin, 1808.

Lacretelle jeune, Charles. *Histoire de France pendant le dix-huitième siècle,* 4 vols. 4th ed. Paris: Delaunay, 1819.

———. *Précis historique de la Révolution Française. Convention Nationale,* 2 vols. Paris: Treuttel et Würtz, 1803.

———. *Precis historique de la Révolution Française. Directoire Exécutif,* 2 vols. Paris: Treuttel et Wurtz, 1806.

La-Varenne, Charles de. *Histoire particulière des événemens qui ont eu lieu en France pendant les mois de juin, juillet, d'août et de septembre 1792.* Paris: Colin, 1806.

Lecomte, P. C. *Mémorial ou Journal Historique impartial et anecdotique de la Révolution de France, contenant une série, exacte des faits principaux qui ont amené et prolongé cette révolution, depuis 1786, jusqu'à l'armistice signé dans les derniers jours de l'an VIII; dans lequel la chronologie a été scrupuleusement observée, et où l'on voit quantité de rapprochemens curieux, d'anecdotes héroiques, nationales et satyriques, la plupart inédites*, 3 vols. Paris: Duponcet, 1801–03.

Lemaire, Nicholas-Eloi. *Virgile expliqué par le Siècle de Napoléon, dans une séance publique du cours de poésie latine*. Paris: 1812.

Lenglet. *Révolutions du Globe*. Paris: Verdière, 1812.

Lenoir, Alexandre. *Description chronologique et historique des status en marbre et en bronze, bas-reliefs et tombeaux des hommes et des femmes célèbres qui sont réunis dans ce Musée*. Paris: Musée impérial des Monumens français, 1811.

————. *Dissertation sur les deux question suivantes: A-t-il existé un tribunal pour juger les rois d'Egypte après leur mort?—Les pyramides d'Egypte étaient-elles destinées à servir de tombeaux aux rois?* Paris: Chanson, 1812.

————. *Histoire de la peinture sur verre, et description des vitraux anciens et modernes, pour servir à l'histoire de l'art relativement à la France, etc.* Paris: 1804.

————. *Nouvelle explication des Hiéroglyphes, ou des Anciennes Allégories sacrées des Egyptiens utile à l'intelligence des Monumens mythologiques des autres peuples*. Paris: Au Musée des monumens français, 1809.

Le Pileur, H. A. *Recherches sur les Lois Constitutionnelles de la France depuis le roi Pharamond jusqu'à l'empereur Napoléon*. Paris: Th. Barrois et Tourneis, 1809.

Leuliette, J.-J. *Discours sur cette question: Comment l'abolition progressive de la Servitude en Europe a-t-elle influé sur le developpement des lumières et des richesses des Nations?* Versailles: Locard, 1805.

Lévesque, Pierre-Chârles. *Histoire critique de la république romaine. Ouvrage dans lequel on s'est proposé de détruire des préjugés invétérés sur l'histoire des premiers siècles de la république, sur la morale des Romains, leurs vertus, leur politique extérieure, leur constitution et le caractére de leurs hommes célèbres*, 3 vols. Paris: Dentu, 1807.

————. *Histoire de Russie*, 8 vols. Hambourg and Brunswick: chez Pierre-François Fauche et Cie, 1800.

Mallet, Paul-Henri. *De la Ligue Hanséatique de son origine, ses progrès, sa puissance et sa constitution politique jusqu'à son déclin au seizième siècle*. Geneva: G.J. Manget, 1805.

Malleville fils, *Discours sur l'influence de la réformation de Luther, ouvrage dont il a été fait mention honorable dans la dernière séance publique l'Institut national*. Paris: Le Normand, 1804.

Matériaux pour servir à l'Histoire 1805–1807. 2nd ed. Paris: Colnet, 1808.

Millot, Abbé, C.-F.-X. *Histoire Générale*. Paris: Costes, 1811.

Moithey, M.-A. *Abrégé de l'histoire de France, depuis Clovis, jusques et y compris le règne de Louis XVI*, 3 vols. Paris: Crapelet, 1810.

Monier, F.-M. *Histoire de Pologne, depuis son origine jusqu'en 1795, Epoque du partage définitif de ce Royaume entre la Russie, la Prusse, et l'Autriche; précédée de détails exacts sur la Géographie, l'Agriculture, le Commerce, l'Instruction, les Moeurs, les Coutumes, et l'ancien Gouvernement des Polonais*, 2 vols. Paris: Fain, 1807.

Montyon, A.J.-B.-R. *Particularités et observations sur les Ministres des Finances de France les plus célèbres depuis 1660 jusqu'en 1791*. Paris: Le Normant, 1812.

Musset-Pathay, V.-D. *Recherches historiques sur le cardinal de Retz; suivies des portraits, pensées et maximes extraits de ses Ouvrages*. Paris: D. Colas, 1807.

———. *Souvenirs historiques ou coup-d'oeil sur les monarchies de l'Europe et sur les causes de leur grandeur ou de leur décadence*. Paris: D. Colas, 1810.

Noël, François. *Dictionnaire historique des personnages célèbres de l'antiquité Princes, Généraux, Philosophes, Poètes, Artistes, etc.; des Dieux, Héros de la Fable; des Villes, Fleuves, etc.* Paris: Nicolle, 1806.

Nougaret, P.-J.-B. *Histoire du Donjon et du Château de Vincennes*, 3 vols. Paris: Brunot-Labbe, 1807.

Paoli-Chagny. *Annales historiques, politiques, civiles, et militaires du dix-neuvième siècle*. Ratzebourg: 1806.

Papon, Jean Pierre. *Tableau d'une Histoire de la Révolution Française*. Paris: 1801.

Pasumot, François. *Dissertations et Mémoires sur differens sujets d'antiquité et d'histoire, avec cartes et gravures, pour servir de suite aux Antiquites de Mr. de Caylus et à celles de Mr. de la Sauvagerre; mis en ordre et publiés par C. M. Grivaud*. Paris: 1810–13.

Peppe, J.-F. *Origine des Francs Saliens*. Anvers: year XIII.

Petit, F. Rouillon. *Essai sur la monarchie française ou Précis de l'Histoire de France*. Paris: Pillet, 1812.

Pièces inédites sur les règnes de Louis XIV, Louis XV et Louis XVI. Paris: Collin, 1809.

Portalis fils. *Du Devoir de l'Historien, de bien considérer le caractère et le génie de chaque siècle en jugeant les grands hommes qui y ont vécu; Discours couronné par l'Académie royale des Inscriptions et Belles-Lettres, Histoire et Antiquités de Stockholm, en mars 1800*. Paris: chez Bernard, year VIII.

Pradt, Dominique Georges Frédéric de Riore de Prolhiac de Fourt de. *Histoire de l'ambassade dans le grand duché de Varsovée en 1812, par M. de Pradt*. . . . Paris: Chez Pillet, 1815.

Proyart, Abbé L.-B. *Louis XVI détrôné avant d'être Roi*. Paris: l'auteur, 1803.

Les Quinze, ou l'Histoire de la Grande Armée. Paris: Obré, 1801.

Rivoire, Maurice. *Précis Historique de la surprise d'Amiens par les espagnols le 11 mars 1597 . . . précédé d'un coup-d'oeil militaire sur le département de la Somme.* Amiens: Maisel, 1806.

Rougeron, P. N. *Le Règne de Charlemagne, roi des Français et Empereur d'Occident.* Paris: Villet, 1807.

Rulhière, Claude Carloman de. *Histoire de l'anarchie de Pologne, et du démembrement de cette république, par Cl. Rulhière. Suivie des anecdotes sur la révolution de Russie, en 1792, par le même auteur,* 4 vols. Paris: Desenne, 1807.

Sacy, A.-I. Baron Silvestre de. *Mélanges de Sacy. Mémoire sur une correspondance inédite entre Tamerlan et le roi de France Charles VI. Lu dans la séance de la Classe d'histoire et de littérature ancienne et l'Institut de France, du vendredi 3 juillet 1812.* Extract from *Le Moniteur,* Nº 226, 1812.

Sade, Louis-Marie de. *Histoire de la Nation française, Première Race.* Paris: Baudouin. 1805.

Saint-Allais, N. Vitron de. *La France Militaire,* 2 vols. Paris: Lepetit, 1812.

———. *Tablettes Chronologiques, généalogiques et historiques.* Paris: Vanraest, 1812.

———. *La Verité rendue sensible à la nation français sur les causes et les effets de la révolution et sur l'administration du premier consul Bonaparte.* Paris: 1803.

Saint-Genois de Grand-Breucq, François-Joseph de. *Monumens anciens,* 2 vols. Paris: Saillant, 1782–1804.

Schoell, Frédéric. *Eléments de chronologie historique.* Paris: chez Fr. Schoell, 1812.

———. *Précis de la Révolution française et des événements Politiques et militaires qui l'ont suivie, jusqu'au 1er avril 1810.* 2nd ed. Paris: F. Schoell, 1810.

Ségur, Louis Philippe. *Histoire des principaux événemens du règne de F. Guillaume II, roi de Prusse, et tableau politique de l'Europe depuis 1786 jusqu'en 1796, ou l'an 4 de la république,* 3 vols. Paris: F. Buisson, 1800.

Sérieys. *Bibliothèque académique ou Choix fait par une Société de Gens-de-Lettres, de différens mémoires des Académies françaises et étrangères, la plupart traduits, pour la première fois, du Latin, de l'Italien, de l'Anglais, etc.,* 12 vols. Paris: Delacour, 1811.

———. *Epigrammes anecdotiques inédites concernant des hommes célèbres.* Paris: Vve Perronneau, 1814.

———. *Epitome de l'Histoire des Papes, depuis saint Pierre jusqu'à nos jours, avec un précis historique de la vie de Pie VII, depuis son élévation au trône pontifical jusqu'à son arrivée à Paris. Ouvrage élémentaire à l'usage de la jeunesse, revu par l'abbé Sicard.* Paris: Hénée, 1804.

――――. *La Fin du 18ᵉ siècle, ou anecdotes curieuses et intéressantes, tirées de manuscrits originaux, de pièces officielles ou transmises par les auteurs mêmes des faits, ou par des témoins non suspects; pour servir de matériaux, et de pièces justicatives, à l'Histoire de la République française, etc.* Paris: Chez Monory, 1805–06.

――――. *Fouché, Sa Vie privée, politique et morale, depuis son entrée à la Convention jusqu'à ce jour.* Paris: Chez Germain Mathiot, 1816.

――――. *Histoire abrégée de la campagne de Napoléon-le-Grand, en Allemagne et en Italie, jusqu'à la paix de Presbourg; avec un exposé des principaux faits depuis ce traité jusqu'au retour de S. M. à sa capitale . . .* Paris: Henée; Demoraine, 1805.

――――. *Histoire de l'Etablissement du Christianisme dans les Indes Orientales.* Paris: Ouvrier, 1803.

――――. *Recherches historiques sur les dignités et leurs marques distinctives chez différens peuples tant anciens que modernes; Suivies de la Loi sur la création de la Légion d'Honneur, et des Décrets impériaux, concernant les rangs, les préséances et les Titres héréditaires.* Paris: Léopold Collin, 1808.

――――. *Les Souvenirs de M. le comte de Caylus.* Paris: Hubert et Cⁱᵉ, 1805.

Sismondi, J.C.L. Simonde de. *Histoire des Républiques italiennes du moyen âge,* 10 vols. New ed. Paris: Furne et Cⁱᵉ, 1840.

Soulavie aîné, J.L. *Mémoires historiques et politiques du règne de Louis XVI, depuis son mariage jusqu'à sa mort; ouvrage composé sur des pièces authentiques fournies à l'auteur avant la révolution, par plusieurs ministres et hommes d'état; et sur les pièces justificatives recueillies, après la 10 Août, dans les cabinets de Louis XVI à Versailles, à Rambouillet et au château des Tuileries,* 6 vols. Paris: Treuttel et Würtz, year X.

Tableau systematique des Archives de l'Empire. Paris: Baudouin, Imp. de l'Institut impérial, 1811.

Toulongeon, F. Emmanuel. *Histoire de France depuis la Révolution de 1789, Ecrites d'après les mémoires et manuscrits contemporains, recueillis dans les dépôts civils et militaires,* 4 vols. Paris: Treuttel et Würtz, 1801–10.

Vauban. *Mémoires pour servir à l'histoire de la Guerre de la Vendée.* Paris: à la Maison de commission en librairie, 1806.

Villers, Charles. *Essai sur l'esprit et l'influence de la réformation de Luther, ouvrage qui a remporté le prix sur cette question proposée dans la séance publique du 25 germinal an X, par l'Institut national de France.* Paris: Henrichs, 1804.

Zinserling, E.A. *Le Système Fédératif des anciens mis en parallèle avec celui des modernes.* Heidelberg: J. Engelmann, 1809.

4. PRINTED DOCUMENTS

Almanach de l'Université impériale, 4 vols. Paris: Brunot-Labbe, Libraire de l'Université impériale, 1810–13.

Almanach national de France. Paris: chez Testu, year IX.

Annuaire de l'instruction publique, 2 vols. Paris: years X–XI.

Beauchamp, Alfred de. *Recueil des lois et règlements sur l'enseignement supérieur*, 5 vols. Paris: Delalain frères, 1880–98.

Circulaire et instructions officielles relatives à l'instruction publique de 1802 à 1900, 12 vols. Paris: 1863–1902.

Duvergier, Jean Baptist, ed. *Collection complète des lois, décrets, ordonnances, règlemens et avis du Conseil d'Etat . . . de 1788 à 1824*, 78 vols. Paris: 1824–78.

Guillaume, James, ed. *Procès-verbaux du Comité d'instruction publique de l'Assemblée législative*. Paris: 1889.

————. ed. *Procès-verbaux du Comité d'instruction publique de la Convention nationale . . .*, 5 vols. Paris: 1891–1907.

Procès-Verbal des Séances du Tribunat, 59 vols. Paris: Imprimerie nationale, year X.

Recueil des lois et règlements concernant l'instruction publique, Ier serie, 4 vols. Paris: publisher not given, 1814; 2nd series. Paris: publisher not given, 1820–28.

Recueil des Lois et règlements concernant l'instruction publique, depuis l'édit de Henri IV, en 1598, jusqu'à ce jour, publié par ordre de Son Excellence le grand-maître de l'Université de France, 4 vols. Paris: Brunot-Lable, 1812–20.

Rendu, Ambroise. *Code universitaire*. Paris: L. Hachette, 1827, 1835, 1846.

5. OTHER PRIMARY WORKS

Aguesseau, M. le Chancelier. *Oeuvres*, 13 vols. Paris: Les Libraires Associés, 1759.

Barnard, H.C. *The Port-Royalists on Education. Extracts from the Educational Writing of the Port-Royalists*. Cambridge: the University Press, 1918.

Barruel, Etienne. *Observations sur l'instruction publique et particulièrement sur les écoles centrales*. Paris: Baudouin, year VIII.

Basset, César-Auguste. *Coup d'oeil générale sur l'éducation et l'instruction publique en France*. Paris: L. Colas, 1816.

Bernard, Samuel. *Discours prononcé par Mr. Samuel Bernard à la distribution solennelle des prix décernés aux élèves du collège de Rochefort le 15 septembre 1810*. Rochefort: Chez Goulard, 1810.

Bidou, Charles. *Le Guide d'une Mère, ou traité d'éducation particulière*, 2 vols. 2nd ed. Paris: Le Normant, 1804.

Blanchard, Abbé Pierre. *Préceptes pour l'éducation des deux sexes à l'usage des familles Chrétiennes . . . redigés et mis en ordre, d'après son manuscrit, par Bruyset aîné, de l'Académie de Lyon, de la Société d'Agriculture et des Arts de la même ville. . . .* Lyons: chez Bruyset aîné et Cie, 1803.

Bonaparte, Joseph. *Mémoires et correspondance politique et militaire du roi Joseph.* Paris: Perrotin, 1855.

Buffier, Claude. *Pratique de la Mémoire artificielle, pour apprendre et pour retenir aisement la chronologie et l'histoire universelle,* 2 vols. Paris: D. Jollet, 1711.

Cambacérès, Jean-Jacques Régis de. *Lettres inédites à Napoléon 1802–1814,* with notes by Jean Tulard, 2 vols. Paris: Editions Klincksieck, 1973.

Campe, Joachim Heinrich. *Bibliothèque de l'enfance,* 2 vols. Paris: Legras et Cordier, 1805.

Capelle, P. *Aneries Révolutionnaires.* Paris: Capelle, 1801.

Chantreau, Pierre-Nicholas, *Manuel des Instituteurs.* Paris: Desenne, year III.

Daniel, G.,S.J. *Histoire de France depuis l'établissement de la monarchie françoise dans les gaules,* 3 vols. Paris: Jean-Baptise Delespine, 1713.

Fénelon, *Education des Filles.* Paris: Librairie des Bibliophiles, 1885.

Fouché, Joseph. *Mémoires de Joseph Fouché, Duc d'Otrante,* 2 vols. 2nd ed. Paris: Le Rouge, 1824.

Gaultier, Abbé Alouisine-Edouard-Camille. *Traits caractéristiques d'une mauvaise éducation.* Paris: A.-A. Renouard, 1812.

Guizot, François, ed. *Annales de l'éducation,* 4 vols. Paris: Le Normant, 1811–14.

———. *Essai sur l'histoire et l'état actuel de l'instruction publique.* Paris: Maradan, 1816.

———. *Mémoires,* 8 vols. Paris: Michel Lévy Frères, 1858–67.

Hauterive, Ernest d'. *La Police Secrète du Premier Empire,* 5 vols. Paris: Librairie académique Perrin, 1908–64.

Herold, J. Christopher, ed. *The Mind of Napoleon.* New York: Columbia University Press, 1955.

Histoire et Mémoires de l'Institut Royal de France, Classe d'Histoire et de Littérature ancienne. Vol. I; Paris: de l'Imprimerie Royale, 1815.

Institut de France. 3e Classe. Travaux divers 1803–1816. Vols. XV–XVII.

Institut Imperial de France. Vol. V; Paris: Chez Firmin Didot, 1812.

Institut National des Sciences et Arts. Vol. II; Paris: Baudouin, year X.

Izarn, Joseph. *Exposé de l'état actuel de l'instruction publique.* Paris: J.G. Dentu, 1815.

Jullien, Marc-Antoine. *Esprit de la méthode d'éducation de Pestalozzi, suivie et pratiquée dans l'Institut d'éducation d'Yverdun, en Suisse,* 2 vols. Milan: Imprimerie royale, 1812.

Journal général de la littérature de France ou Répertoire methodique des livres nouveaux, cartes géographiques, estampes et oeuvres de musique qui paraissent successivement en France, accompagné de notes analytiques et critiques, 44 vols. Paris-Strasbourg: Treuttel et Würtz, 1798–1841.

Lavallée, Joseph. *Annales nécrologiques de la Légion d'honneur . . .*, 2 vols. Paris: chez F. Buisson, 1807.

Lebrun, Isidore. *De l'Instruction publique sous Napoléon et de l'Université.* Paris: Gide Fils, 1814.

Lecestre, Léon, ed. *Lettres inédites de Napoléon Ier*, 2 vols. 2nd ed. Paris: Plon, 1897.

Legroing La Maisonneuve, Antoinette. *Essai sur le genre d'Instruction qui paroît le plus analogue à la destination des Femmes.* Paris: Dufart, year 7.

———. *Essai sur l'Instruction des Femmes.* 3rd ed. Tours: R. Pornin, 1844.

Le Moniteur universel. Paris: Agasse, 1789–1830.

Liste des Membres et des Correspondans de l'Institut avec les Changemens arrivés depuis le 1er Janvier 1807, jusqu'au 1er Janvier 1808. Vol. IV; Paris: Baudouin, 1808.

Napoleon I, Emperor. *Correspondance de Napoléon Ier publiée par ordre de l'Empereur Napoléon III*, 32 vols. Paris: Henri Plon, 1858–70.

Organisation et Réglemens de l'Institut National. Vol. III; Paris: Baudouin, 1805.

Pelet de la Lozère, Joseph. *Opinions de Napoléon sur divers sujets de politique et d'administration recueillies par un membre de son conseil d'état, et récit de quelques événemens de l'époque.* Paris: Firmin Didot Frères, 1833.

Petau, Père Dennis. *Abrégé chronologique de l'Histoire universelle sacrée et profane. Traduction nouvelle.* Paris: Barbin, 1708.

Rémusat, Paul de, ed. *Mémoirs of Madame de Rémusat.* 1802–1808. New York: D. Appleton and Company, 1880.

Rendu, Ambroise. *Essai sur l'instruction publique*, 3 vols. Paris: A. Egron, 1819.

Roger. *Discours prononcé par M. Roger, en présentant au Corps Législatif l'hommage que fait M. Lacretelle, jeune, des deux premiers volumes de son Histoire de France pendant le 18e siècle. Séance du 14 decembre 1808.* Paris: Corps législatif, 1808.

Sérieys, Antoine. *Chefs-d'oeuvre d'eloquence tirés des ourvres de Bossuet, Fléchier, Fontenelle et Thomas. Adoptés par le Gouvernement, pour la classe des belles-lettres, dans les lycées et ecoles secondaires.* Paris: Obré, 1806.

Staël-Holstein, Anne Louise Germaine. *Considerations sur les Principaux Evénements de la Révolution Française.* London: Baldwin, Cradock and Joy, 1818.

Table des Matières des noms de lieux et des noms de personnes. Paris: l'imprimerie nationale, year XIV.

Tableau systématique des Archives de l'Empire, 15 août 1811. Paris: Baudouin, Imp. de l'Institut impériale.

Tableau systématique des Archives de l'Empire. Paris: Baudouin, Imp. de l'Institut impériale, 1811.

Tessonneau, Rémy, ed. *Fontanes, Correspondance de Louis de Fontanes et Joseph Joubert*. Paris: 1943.

Thierry, Augustin. *Récits des Temps Merovingiens, précédés de considerations sur l'Histoire de France*, 2 vols. Paris: Librairie de Firmin-Didot et Cie, 1883.

Vox, Maximilien. *Bonaparte me Disait . . . Conversations notées par le comte P.L. Roederer*. Paris: Horizons de France, 1942.

Wandelcourt, Hubert. *L'Ecole de la Vertu et de la Politesse, ouvrage destiné aux petites Ecoles des Villes et des campagnes*. Paris: Collin, 1808.

————. *Le Mentor ou Le Livre des Demoiselles*. Paris: Collin, 1808.

————. *Le Mentor ou Le Livre des Demoiselles*. Breslau: Guillaume Théophile Korn, 1809.

————. *Plan d'Education et d'Instruction publique*. Paris: Fournier, 1801.

6. REFERENCE WORKS

Bibliographie de la France; ou Journal général de l'imprimerie et de la librairie, annual. Paris: Au Cercle de la librairie, November 1811–1929.

Biographie des Grands Hommes et des Personnages Remarquables qui ont vécu sous l'empire. Paris: Eugène et Victor Penaud Frères, 1852.

Biographie Moderne, ou dictionnaire biographique de tous les hommes morts et vivants qui ont marqué à la fin du XVIIIe siècle et au commencement de celui-ci par leur écrits, 2 vols. Paris: A. Eymery, 1815.

Biographie Universelle Ancienne et Moderne, 85 vols. Paris: Michaud, 1811–62.

Biographie Universelle (Michaud), Nouvelle edition, 45 vols. Paris: Chez Madame C. Desplaces, 1843–65.

Dezobry, Charles, Th. Bachelet et al. *Dictionnaire général de Biographie et d'Histoire . . .*, 2 vols. Paris: Librairie Charles Delagrave, 1880.

Fierville, Charles. *Archives et Bibliographie des lycées*. Paris: 1893.

Grand Dictionnaire universel du XIXe siècle par Pierre Larousse. Paris: Administration du grand dictionnaire universel, 1876.

La Grande Encyclopédie. Paris: H. Lamirault, 1886–1902.

Monglond, André. *La France révolutionnaire et impériale*, 9 vols. Grenoble: Editions B. Arthaud, 1930.

Quérard, Joseph-Marie. *La France littéraire . . .*, 12 vols. Paris: F. Didot père et fils, 1827–39.

Universal Prounouncing Dictionary of Biography and Mythology. 4th ed. Philadelphia: Lippincott, 1915.

7. SECONDARY WORKS

Allen, Annie Winsor. "Pierre-Louis Roederer (1754–1835) Sa vie et son oeuvre." Ph.D. diss., Faculté des Lettres de l'Université de Paris, 1958.

Artz, Friedrich B. "L'Enseignement technique en France pendant l'époque révolutionnaire, 1789–1815," *Revue Historique*, CXCV (July, 1946), 257–86 and 385–407.

Aulard, François Victor Alphonse. *Napoléon Ier et le monopole universitaire.* Paris: A. Colin, 1911.

————. "Premiers Historiens de la Révolution française," *Etudes et leçons sur la Révolution française*, VI (1910), 32–134.

Bardoux, M.A. *Guizot.* Paris: Hachette et Cie, 1894.

Barnard, H.C. *The French Tradition in Education.* Cambridge: University Press, 1922.

————. *The Little Schools of Port-Royal.* Cambridge: University Press, 1913.

Berthier, Ferdinand. *L'Abbé Sicard, célèbre instituteur des sourdsmuets, précis historique sur sa vie ses travaux et ses succès.* Paris: Douniol et Cie, 1873.

Bonnel. *La Réorganisation de l'instruction publique en 1802.* Lyon: A. Rey, 1894.

Boudart, René. *L'Organisation de l'Université et de l'enseignement secondaire dans l'Académie Impériale Gênes 1805 et 1814.* Paris: Mouton, 1962.

Bourgeois, Emile. *La Liberté d'Enseignement: Histoire et Doctrine.* Paris: Edouard Cornely, 1902.

Buisson, Henry. *Fouché duc d'Otrante.* Bienne, Switzerland: Editions du Panorama, 1968.

Charmot, F., S.J. *La Pédagogie des Jésuites—Ses principes—Son actualité.* Paris: Editions Spes, 1943.

Charpentier, John. *Napoléon et les hommes de lettres de son temps.* Paris: Mercure de France, 1935.

Compayré, Gabriel. *Histoire Critique des Doctrines de l'Education en France depuis le seizième siècle*, 2 vols. 5th ed. Paris: Librairie Hachette et Cie, 1885.

Cornuz, Jeanlouis. *Jules Michelet un aspect de la pensée religieuse au XIXe siècle.* Geneva: Librairie E. Droz, 1955.

Daniel, Charles. *Les Jésuites Instituteurs de la Jeunesse Française au XVIIe et au XVIIIe siècle.* Paris: Société Général de Librairie Catholique, 1880.

Dupont-Ferrier, Gustave. *Du Collège de Clermont au Lycée Louis-le Grand (1563–1920).* Paris: E. de Boccard, 1925.

Durand, C. *L'Exercice de la Fonction législative de* 1800 *à* 1814. Aix-en-Provence: 1955.

Durand, R. "Le Monopole universitaire et la concurrence ecclésiastique dans les Côtes-du-Nord" *Revue d'Histoire moderne*, (1934), 16–47.

Durkheim, Emile. *L'Evolution pédagogique en France*. Paris: Librairie Felix Alcan, 1938.

Edmond-Blanc, Amédée. *Napoléon Ier Ses Institutions Civiles et Administratives*. Paris: E. Plon et Cie, 1880.

Falcucci, Cl. *L'Humanisme, dans l'enseignement secondaire en France au XIXe siècle*. Paris: 1939.

Faure, Elie. *Napoleon*. New York: Alfred A. Knopf, 1924.

Fisher, H.A.L. *Napoleon*. 2nd ed. London: Oxford University Press, 1967.

Franklin, Julian H. *Jean Bodin and the Sixteenth Century Revolution in the Methodology of Law and History*. New York and London: Columbia University Press, 1963.

Gal, R. *Histoire de l'éducation*. Paris: Presses Universitaire, 1966.

Godechot, Jacques. *Les Institutions de la France sous la Révolution et l'Empire*. Paris: Presses Universitaires, 1951.

Gontard, Maurice. *L'Enseignement Primaire en France de la Révolution à la loi Guizot* (1789–1833). Paris: Société d'Editions "Les Belles Lettres".

Gooch, G.P. *History and Historians in the Nineteenth Century*. Boston: Beacon Press, 1959.

Gréard, Octave. *Histoire critique des doctrines de l'éducation en France depuis le XVIe siècle jusqu'à nos jours*. Paris: impr. de E. Colas, 1877.

———. *La Législation de L'Instruction Primaire en France depuis* 1789 *jusqu'à nos jours*. Paris: Charles de Mourques Frères, 1874.

Grimaud, Louis. *Histoire de la liberté d'enseignement en France depuis la chute de l'ancien régime jusqu'en nos jours*. Paris: 1898.

Guigue, A. *La Faculté des Lettres de l'Université de Paris, depuis sa fondation* (17 *mars* 1808) *jusqu'au Ier janvier* 1935. Paris: 1935.

Hippeau, C. *L'Instruction Publique en France Pendant la Révolution*. Paris: Didier et Cie, 1881.

Holtman, Robert. *Napoleonic Propaganda*. Baton Rouge: Louisiana State University Press, 1950.

Huppert, George, "The New History of the French Renaissance," Ph.D. diss., the University of California, Berkeley, 1962.

———. "The Renaissance Background of Historicism," *History and Theory*, V (No. 1, 1966), 48–60.

Johnson, Douglas. *Guizot*. London: Routledge, 1963.

Jourdain, Charles. *Histoire de l'Université de Paris*. Paris: Hachette, 1866.

Jullien, Camille Louis. *Extraits des Historiens français du XIXe siècle*. Paris: Librairie Hachette et Cie, 1897.

Kinser, Samuel C. "The Historiography of J.A. de Thou," Ph.D. diss., Cornell University, 1960.

Koechlin, H. *Compétence administrative et judiciaire de 1800 à 1830*. Paris: 1951.

Lanzac de Laborie. "La Haute administration de l'enseignement sous le Consulat et l'Empire," *Revue des études napoléoniennes*, II (1916), 186–219.

Latappy, J. "L'Eglise et l'Université sous Napoléon Ier," *Correspondant*, CCIII (1909), 1924–38.

Lavallée, Théophile. *Histoire de la Maison Royale de Saint-Cyr* (1686–1793). Paris: Furne et Cie, 1853.

Léon, Antoine. "Promesses et Ambiguités de l'oeuvre d'enseignement technique en France, de 1800 à 1815," *Revue d'histoire moderne et contemporaine*, XVII (July–September, 1970), 846–59.

Le Poittevin, Georges. *La Liberté de la presse depuis la révolution, 1789–1815*. Paris: A. Rousseau, 1901.

Letaconnoux, M.J., ed. *La Lutte Scolaire en France au dix-neuvième siècle*. Paris: Librairie Felix Alcan, 1912.

Liard, L. *L'Enseignement supérieur en France 1789–1893*, 2 vols. Paris: A. Colin, 1888–94.

Madelin, Louis. *Histoire du Consulat et de l'Empire*, 16 vols. Paris: Hachette, 1948.

Mellon, Stanley, *The Political Uses of History*. Stanford, California, Stanford University Press, 1958.

Morange, Jean and Jean-François Chassaing. *Le Mouvement de réforme de l'enseignement en France 1760–1798*. Paris: Presses Universitaires de France, 1974.

Pariset, Georges. *Le Consulat et l'Empire*. Vol. III of *Histoire de France contemporaine*. Edited by Ernest Lavisse. 10 vols. Paris: Librairie Hachette, 1921.

Parker, Harold T. *The Cult of Antiquity and the French Revolutionaries*. Chicago: University of Chicago Press, 1937.

———. "The Formation of Napoleon's Personality: An Exploratory Essay," *French Historical Studies* VII (Spring, 1971), 6–26.

Paucton-Grasset, Michelle. "La Pédagogie familiale de l'époque Napoléonienne (1800–1815)," *Revue de l'Institut Napoléon*, CIV (July 1967), 117–29.

Pearce, William L. "Science, Education and Napoleon I," *Isis*, (1956), 369–82.

Peyre, Henri. "Napoleon: Devil, Poet, Saint," *Yale French Studies*, (No. 26, 1960–61), 21–31.

Ponteil, F. *Napoléon Ier et l'organisation autoritaire de la France*. Paris: Colin, 1966.

Reinhard, Marcel. *La Légende de Henry IV*. Saint-Brieuc: Les Presses Bretonnes, 1935.

Reval, Gabrielle. *Madame Campan Assistante de Napoléon*. Paris: Albin Michel Editeur, 1931.

Riancey, Henri de. *Histoire critique et législative d'instruction publique et de la Liberté de l'enseignement en France*, 2 vols. Paris: Sagnier et Bray, 1844.

Rigault, G. *Histoire générale de l'Institut des frères des écoles chrétiennes*. Paris: 1940.

Schmidt, Charles. *La Réforme de l'Université impériale en 1811*. Paris: G. Bellais, 1905.

Scott, Barbara. "Madame Campan," *History Today*, XXIII (No. 10, October 1973), 683–90.

Simon, René. "Un lycée sous l'empire; le lycée de Poitiers," *Revue des études napoléoniennes*, VII (1915), 324–40.

Smith, Agnes Monroe. "The First Historians of the French Revolution." Ph.D. diss., Western Reserve University, 1966.

Snyders, Georges. *La Pédagogie en France aux XVIIe et XVIIIe siècles*. Paris: Presses Universitaires de France, 1965.

Stadler, Peter. *Geschichtschreibung und historische Denken in Frankreich 1789–1871*. Zurich: Verlag Berichthaus, 1958.

Stenger, Gilbert. *La Société française pendant le Consulat*. Paris: 1903–08.

Tessonneau, Remy. *Joubert*. Paris: 1944.

Thompson, James Westfall. *A History of Historical Writing*, 2 vols. New York: Macmillan, 1942.

Tomiche, Nada. *Napoléon Ecrivain*. Paris: Librairie Armand Colin, 1952.

Welschinger, Henri. *La Censure sous le premier empire*. Paris: Perrin et Cie, 1887.

Wilson, Aileen. *Fontanes: Essai Biographique et Littéraire*. Paris: E. de Boccard, 1928.

Young, Norwood. *The Growth of Napoleon: A Study in Environment*. London: John Murray, 1910.